BEING DEAF

INTRODUCTION TO BLOCK 1

UNIT 2
THE DEAF COMMUNITY
PREPARED FOR THE COURSE TEAM BY JIM KYLE

UNIT 3
BRITISH SIGN LANGUAGE, COMMUNICATION AND DEAFNESS
PREPARED FOR THE COURSE TEAM BY SUSAN GREGORY AND DOROTHY MILES

PAINTING ON COVER AND TITLE PAGE BY TREVOR LANDELL

The Open University

THIS COURSE HAS BEEN PRODUCED WITH FUNDING FROM THE DEPARTMENT OF HEALTH

D251 Core Course Team

ANNE DARBY Diploma Placements Officer, Faculty of Social Sciences

SUSAN GREGORY Senior Lecturer in Psychology, Faculty of Social Sciences (Course Team Chair)

YVONNE HOLMES Secretary, Faculty of Social Sciences

LINDA JANES Course Manager, Faculty of Social Sciences

GEORGE TAYLOR Lecturer in Interdisciplinary Social Sciences, Faculty of Social Sciences

Other Open University Contributors

JULIET BISHOP Research Fellow in Social Sciences, Faculty of Social Sciences

DEBBIE CROUCH Designer

TIM DANT Research Fellow in Health and Social Welfare, Continuing Education

VIC FINKELSTEIN Senior Lecturer in Health and Social Welfare, Continuing Education

GERALD HALES Research Fellow, Institute of Educational Technology

FIONA HARRIS Editor

KEITH HOWARD Graphic Artist

MARY JOHN Senior Lecturer in Psychology, Faculty of Social Sciences

VIC LOCKWOOD BBC Producer

KEN PATTON BBC Producer

ALISON TUCKER BBC Producer

External Consultants

LORNA ALLSOP Centre for Deaf Studies, University of Bristol

LARAINE CALLOW Consultant in Deafness

MARY FIELDER National Council of Social Workers with Deaf People

GILLIAN M. HARTLEY Teacher, Thorn Park School, Bradford

LYNNE HAWCROFT Royal National Institute for the Deaf

JIM KYLE Centre for Deaf Studies, University of Bristol

PADDY LADD London Deaf Video Project

CARLO LAURENZI National Deaf Children's Society

CLIVE MASON Presenter, BBC 'See Hear'

RUKHSANA MEHERALI Educational Psychologist, Royal School for the Deaf, Derby

DOROTHY MILES Writer, Lecturer and Poet

BOB PECKFORD British Deaf Association

CHRISTINE PLAYER Tutor Adviser

SHARON RIDGEWAY National Council of Social Workers with Deaf People

JANICE SILO Teacher of the Deaf, Derbyshire

External Assessors

MARY BRENNAN Co-director, MA and Advanced Diploma in Sign Language Studies, University of Durham

MALCOLM PAYNE Head of Department of Applied Community Studies, Manchester Polytechnic

Sign Language Interpreters

BYRON CAMPBELL

ELIZABETH JONES

KYRA POLLITT

LINDA RICHARDS

The Open University
Walton Hall, Milton Keynes
MK7 6AB

First published 1991

Copyright © 1991 The Open University

Designed by the Graphic Design Group of the Open University

Printed in the United Kingdom by The Open University

ISBN 0 7492 0048 0

This publication forms part of the Open University course *D251 Issues in Deafness*. If you have not enrolled on the course and would like to buy this or other Open University material, please write to Open University Educational Enterprises Ltd, 12 Cofferidge Close, Stony Stratford, Milton Keynes MK11 1BY, United Kingdom. If you wish to enquire about enrolling as an Open University student, please write to the Admissions Office, The Open University, P.O. Box 48, Walton Hall, Milton Keynes MK7 6AB, United Kingdom.

Introduction to Block 1

In the three units of this block you are asked to consider various aspects of the lives of deaf people. In Unit 1 you were introduced to individual deaf people, through the personal accounts in Reader One and the Deaf family on Video One. The way in which deaf people are portrayed in society was discussed, and you were asked to reflect upon your own attitudes to deafness.

This block asks you to consider 'Being Deaf' in the context of the community of Deaf people, its culture and its language.

Unit 2 focuses on the Deaf community in the United Kingdom and asks what it is that distinguishes the Community and what it means to belong. Through a description of the history of Deaf people, the structure of their community, their culture, traditions and customs, the unit aims to provide an account of the integrity of Deaf people's lives.

Unit 3 looks at a particular feature of the Community, its language, British Sign Language. It is only in the recent past that this has been fully recognized as a language with its own structure and syntax. The potential of the language is shown by descriptions of its use in a variety of contexts: informal conversations, formal lectures, poetry, humour and debate. The unit considers the implications of the recognition of British Sign Language by examining, in general terms, the relationship between the status of a language and the status of its users.

Unit 4 analyses the notion of a Deaf community further by considering those deaf people who, for whatever reason, may be outside the mainstream of the Deaf community. It takes as examples Black deaf people, gay deaf people, deaf-blind people, older deaf people and oral deaf people, all of whom stand in differing relationships to the mainstream Deaf community. It asks what is the nature of this 'otherness' and from where do these deaf people gain their identity. It finishes by looking at deaf people whose education has precluded sign language, and who are not part of the Deaf community. In discussing the attitudes and feelings of this group, it anticipates some of the arguments in Block 2 which examines Deaf people in hearing worlds.

Unit 2 The Deaf Community

prepared for the course team by Jim Kyle

Contents

Associated study materials

Video One, *Sandra's Story: The History of a Deaf Family.*

Video Two, *Sign Language.*

Reader One, Article 10, 'Making Plans for Nigel: The Erosion of Identity by Mainstreaming', Paddy Ladd.

continued

Reader One, Article 31, 'Acquired Hearing Loss—Acquired Oppression', Maggie Woolley.

Reader Two, Article 1.2, 'Everyone Here Spoke Sign Language', Nora Groce.

Reader Two, Article 2.1, 'Outsiders in a Hearing World', Paul Higgins.

Reader Two, Article 2.3, 'The Modern Deaf Community', Paddy Ladd.

Reader Two, Article 2.4, 'The Deaf Community and the Culture of Deaf People', Carol Padden.

Reader Two, Article 5.10, 'Challenging Conceptions of Integration', Tony Booth.

Reader Two, Article 5.11, 'The Mainstreaming of Primary Age Deaf Children', Susan Gregory and Juliet Bishop.

Set Book: J. Kyle and B. Woll, *Sign Language: The Study of Deaf People and Their Language* (particularly Chapter 1).

D251 Issues in Deafness

Unit 1   *Perspectives on Deafness: An Introduction*

Block 1   Being Deaf
Unit 2   *The Deaf Community*
Unit 3   *British Sign Language, Communication and Deafness*
Unit 4   *The Other Deaf Community?*

Block 2   Deaf People in Hearing Worlds
Unit 5   *Education and Deaf People: Learning to Communicate or Communicating to Learn?*
Unit 6   *The Manufacture of Disadvantage*
Unit 7   *Whose Welfare?*

Block 3   Constructing Deafness
Unit 8   *The Social Construction of Deafness*
Unit 9   *Deaf People as a Minority Group: The Political Process*
Unit 10   *Deaf Futures*

Readers
Reader One: Taylor, G. and Bishop, J. (eds) (1990) *Being Deaf: The Experience of Deafness*, London, Pinter Publishers.
Reader Two: Gregory, S. and Hartley, G.M. (eds) (1990) *Constructing Deafness*, London, Pinter Publishers.

Set Books
Kyle, J. and Woll, B. (1985) *Sign Language: The Study of Deaf People and Their Language*, Cambridge, Cambridge University Press.
Miles, D. (1988) *British Sign Language: A Beginner's Guide*, London, BBC Books (BBC Enterprises). With a chapter by Paddy Ladd.

Videotapes
Video One   *Sandra's Story: The History of a Deaf Family*
Video Two   *Sign Language*
Video Three *Deaf People and Mental Health*
Video Four *Signs of Change: Politics and the Deaf Community*

Aims and objectives

In this unit we will consider the Deaf community and its members with the specific aim of providing a description which will inform our interaction with Deaf people in professional and social situations. The unit is intended to develop topics raised in Unit 1 and should begin to answer some of the questions arising from the activities of Unit 1. You will find the articles in Reader One useful in relation to this unit.

Community, culture and language are closely bound together in the daily lives of Deaf people and trying to describe these features on paper creates certain problems. The first and most serious is the tendency to believe that, once it is written, we have the definitive version of Deaf affairs. Communities change rapidly and descriptions valid on one day in one part of the community may not encompass differences and varying rates of change in other parts of the community. This unit is therefore only a first attempt, a base from which to explore, an invitation for you to go into the Community of Deaf people and to find out for yourselves.

A second problem is the fact that this account is written down and therefore not expressed in the language of the Community. It is perfectly appropriate for people from one culture to describe the way in which another community functions (we have to be clear on that). However, such a description loses some of the rationale and purpose of the culture which would be expressed in the native language of that community. Deaf people may describe themselves differently and offer some different explanations of features described here—that is part of the richness of culture and should not be treated as right or wrong. Culture and community are to be explored and enjoyed. The aim in this unit is to make that access to the Deaf community a little easier.

By the end of the unit you should be able to:

1   Define your own attitudes towards people described as disabled, handicapped and deviant.

2   Discriminate between different groups of people within the Deaf community and between different groups of people who have a hearing loss.

3   Describe the good motives of hearing people which have somehow led society into a situation of decision-making for Deaf people and into a position where such decisions are damaging to their well-being and may even be actively opposed by Deaf people.

4   Understand the reasons why education has borne the brunt of such criticism and analyse the extent to which social work situations may suffer from a similar lack of consultation with Deaf people.

5   Describe the 'construction' of the Deaf community and discuss the question of a Deaf homeland.

6   Describe some of the characteristics of Deaf people who are members of the Community—in terms of the requirements for membership as well as the socio-economic and employment characteristics of the members.

7   Discuss the reasons for not joining the Community, or for the rejection of some people as members, and also the conditions under which one may be able to 'resign' from the Community.

8   Describe the social structure of the Community as seen in inter-club and national activities.

9   Understand the differences shown by those who *acquire* a hearing loss.

10   Distinguish in descriptions of Deaf culture the features of behaviour, custom and tradition which make up the Deaf experience.

11   Contrast the Deaf identity as distinct from the hearing identity and describe the dimension of deafness–hearingness.

12   Summarize the principal aspects of Deaf life which create the culture of deafness.

1 The Deaf community: beginning to believe

> If the laws of heredity that are known to hold in the case of animals also apply to man, the intermarriage of congenital deaf mutes through a number of successive generations should result in the formation of a deaf variety of the human race.
>
> (Alexander Graham Bell, 1884, p. 4)

Despite the apparently ridiculous claims about the transformation of the world in a few generations, there remains a resistance in society and a general uneasiness about the existence of groups of Deaf people and especially about their coming together for social and emotional reasons. Yet perhaps the most powerful factor in the development of any individual is the need to identify others with similar characteristics and with similar experiences. In a world which is very intolerant of difference and where oppression of one group or nation by another is the norm, the position of one group who are ostensibly 'handicapped' or 'less useful members of society' is a very difficult one indeed. We can set out the issue in two ways: Deaf people are either part of a handicapped group or else they are part of a largely unrecognized minority group—but either way they are 'losers' as far as our society in the UK is concerned.

Such a stark diagnosis may seem rather off-putting at the beginning of this course and in a unit which will eventually leave you with a more positive view of the capabilities of Deaf people and with a Deaf perspective on how society works. However, it is as well to address our own socialization and beliefs very early.

 ◀ Activity 1
In Unit 1 you began to consider your own reasons for studying deafness. Jot down a few notes on why you chose this course. ◀

We will need to begin to identify the skills and gifts which only deafness can bring. If we cannot begin to see the advantages of being Deaf and the worth of deafness, then we will, as in other courses and other societies, adopt a patronizing and pseudo-helpful attitude towards the perceived needs of Deaf people. This unit invites you to reappraise your beliefs about deafness.

Deafness is a problem—especially for all the hearing people who choose to come in contact with Deaf people. The level of training provided to our professionals makes them singularly unprepared to cope with Deaf people. The role of the professions in the creation of Deaf handicap can be seen as a major one and one which we have rarely chosen to understand.

◀ Activity 2

Write down a list of trained professionals you think would come into contact with Deaf people in the course of their jobs. Consider for a moment the amount of training they are likely to have had about the topic of deafness and the amount of contact they might have had with Deaf people. Note also if you can how many of these professions have Deaf practitioners. ◀

◀ Comment

You would almost certainly list teachers, social workers, audiologists, doctors and maybe speech therapists. Most have had some training on the topic of deafness but only in the case of teachers of the deaf is it mandatory. Most of these professions make it difficult for Deaf people to be practitioners. None of them requires that practitioners be able to demonstrate that they can communicate with Deaf people. ◀

One of the cornerstone professions of our western society is the medical profession. The job done by a doctor in particular is highly prized. After long training, a doctor is able to interpret the signs of illness and offer remedies; such remedies are at the heart of the belief system of the medical endeavour. Illness is an invasion of the body, an unintended change which leaves the individual feeling less than whole. Such feelings may be very serious and be manifest in obvious signs of physical discomfort, and these physical effects, of course, may be so severe as to threaten life itself. The highest task of the medical profession is to preserve life.

However, problems arise when medical decisions have to be applied to difference rather than to illness. Individuals in society have features which make them different from each other. Even family members are different physically and in temperament. At what point do these differences become so noticeable that they get in the way of what we understand to be 'normal' functioning in everyday life? Superficial physical differences (such as in clothes and physique) tend to be acceptable (though this was not always so). We tend to draw the line where physical functioning is threatened in some way. Particularly vulnerable are the senses, especially those of sight and hearing. So important do these seem to be that problems of sight or hearing are always the first to create attention in emerging educational systems. Only later do we become aware of other physical and then 'mental' problems.

Society's reaction is usually to try to eradicate the difference. This has usually meant recourse to the medical profession in the search for a cure.

But the difference now becomes an abnormality and with it goes the belief that these 'unfortunate' people desire to be part of the wholeness which constitutes the 'normal' society. This view has been reinforced by the numbers of able-bodied people who have acquired a disability and who proclaim extensively about their loss.

Sometimes we choose to highlight those who 'overcome' their difference. This usually means that they carry out acts which deny their specific differences and which can be described as 'despite their problem they ...'. Such acts might be epitomized by Deaf musicians or blind hang-gliders or pilots with no legs.

 ◀ Activity 3
Review your response to the newspaper articles activity in Unit 1. How would you describe your attitudes to Deaf people in the media? ◀

In creating these images of disability, society assumes that all people would be the same (i.e. able-bodied) if they could and that it is the duty of our professions to remedy the situation of those who have a disability or to care for them if their disability proves stubborn. Doctors may try to prevent and then to alter the state; teachers may attempt to offer 'normal' models for the children to emulate and in doing so highlight the perceived 'faults' of their current condition. Employers may try to find a situation which is suited to the perceived limitations of the person rather than offering career enhancement or extension; social workers in the past have also attempted to facilitate the perceived need for normality (Sainsbury, 1986).

The role of teachers has been attacked frequently. It seems that special education has accepted the medical model of 'fixing' the abnormality. The lack of contact and involvement with the real issues has been seen repeatedly by Deaf people:

> Unfortunately few of these educators have intimately mingled with, or made the slightest effort to know, the 'grass-roots' deaf adults; they are normally ignorant of what is going on in the adult deaf world. In all the years which I have spent in the deaf community, which means most of my life, I have noted the presence of hearing educators in the local club of the deaf probably less than five times. However, they do occasionally attend the more salubrious church charity and state association affairs.
>
> (Jacobs, 1980, pp. 19–30)

This professional superiority and aloofness in the name of the normality of hearing society is deeply resented by Deaf people, and one can examine the function of social work services in the past in a similar way.

If we are to have any meaningful assessment of Deaf people and their Community, we have to set aside many of the values and beliefs which seemed so obvious and ingrained. If we do not, we have no way of learning nor of truly experiencing what the Deaf community is and how Deaf culture functions. When we try to learn French or German, we find the most productive experiences are where we learn in the context of the language users themselves. It is through this language experience that we begin to understand the participants in that society. In learning foreign languages we start from a view that members of that culture are equal to ourselves. In entering that culture we lose our identity to some extent because our usual beliefs are suspended for a time and we have little to fall back on and little to guide us until we have mastered the new language. This is also true in Deaf society. You do not 'have to be Deaf to understand' but you do have to be able to question some of these ingrained beliefs about deafness and the 'needs' of Deaf people before you start to learn. If you can begin to do this, then it will be possible to gain much from this course and to begin to enter the world of deafness with a positive and enabling perspective.[1]

2 A brief word on terminology

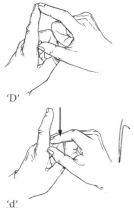

'D'

'd'

Figure 2.1

As was described in Unit 1, there has recently been an attempt to identify Deaf people (with a capital 'D') as distinct from deaf people (with a small 'd'). Small 'd' deaf people are all those who have a hearing loss but who may choose to identify more with the hearing community in language and interaction. Small 'd' deaf may be used occasionally to mean all people with a hearing loss from birth or early childhood. Capital 'D' Deaf people are part of a social grouping whose members share similar experiences and who have usually been educated in contact with groups of other deaf children. What is implied here is that Deaf people share a similar background and from this comes an identity and socialization. This, in turn, implies a 'cultural deafness'. For the moment, Deaf people are those who have, through their experience and background, made a choice to associate with others from a similar situation. This is the weak definition of the Deaf community. By the end of the unit we will have established the strong definition of the Deaf community.

However, as you will have noticed from the above, the distinction of capital 'D' and small 'd' feels very clumsy in spoken and in written English. The reason for this is that it is a distinction which is best made in sign. In Figure 2.1 you can see that capital 'D' is the natural finger-spelled letter 'D', while small 'd' implies a diminution of the concept to a small, even tiny, form of deafness. The visual imagery is what is most powerful here and this does not translate particularly well into capital and small letters in English. However, it remains a useful distinction.

Since 'community' is one of the key terms we wish to use in relation to Deaf people, it is worth pausing a little longer so that you might become clear in your own minds as to the meaning of the term. Padden (1980a) sets out the definition of George Hillery (1974) who had surveyed a range of conceptions of the term:

[1] If you are interested in following up discussion of the emerging views of those who were previously classified as disabled, this can be found in Thomas (1982), Abberley (1987), Barton (1989a,b) and Brechin and Walmsley (1989).

1 A community is a group of people who share common goals and cooperate in achieving these goals. Each community has its own goals. A goal may be equal employment opportunities, greater political participation, or better community services.

2 A community occupies a particular geographical location. The geography of a community determines the ways in which the community functions.

3 A community has some degree of freedom to organize the social life and responsibilities of its members. Institutions such as prisons and mental hospitals bring together groups of people in one locality, but the people have no power to make decisions about their daily lives and routines. Thus we cannot call these types of groups 'communities'.

(Padden, 1980a, p. 3)

◀ Activity 4
Stop for a moment and write a list of the communities of which you feel you are a member. These might be geographical, or local, or be for a specific purpose, or they could be cultural. ◀

This type of definition seems rather traditional and does not adequately characterize the complexities of modern-day life. Padden's own definition is perhaps more appropriate:

A community ... is a general social system in which a group of people live together, share common goals and carry out certain responsibilities to each other.

(Ibid., p. 4)

Yet this is not an adequate view of modern life in a westernized society. Luckman (1970) points out that the traditional communities are less appropriate for the industrialized world we live in. The notion of a community fits uneasily in our everyday existence and is somehow displaced as a tag to give to more primitive situations. She says:

Instead of being a full-time member of one 'total and whole' society, modern man is a part-time citizen in a variety of part-time societies. Instead of living within one meaningful world system to which he owes complete loyalty he now lives in many differently structured 'worlds' to each of which he owes only partial allegiance. Most of modern man's existential universes are single-purpose communities.

(Luckman, 1970, p. 317)

For many people the idea of a community has now become rather alien and the loyalty necessary for participation in community life is rather weak. It can be confined to barbecues or village fêtes as aspects of 'community life', but the commitment of the individual varies very markedly. Because of easy transportation, the locational argument about communities does not work either, since people living in close proximity may manifest no mutual loyalty whatsoever and may exist in very different 'everyday life worlds'.

◀ Activity 5
Looking back at the list you made in Activity 4, decide which communities demand a sense of loyalty and which are simply clubs or single-purpose entities. Can you see how the Deaf community might be a little different? ◀

Perhaps this is why it has become so difficult for hearing people to understand the nature of Deaf society where commitment and participation are stronger and where there is clearly more than a 'single-purpose community'. This lack of comprehension of what a Deaf 'community' might be like is one of the themes which will re-emerge as we examine Deaf people's interaction with each other and can be discerned in Unit 7 which examines the history of welfare services. I believe that succeeding generations of workers in the field have failed to understand the strength and vitality of the Deaf community and have virtually never utilized its skills.

3 Contrasting views on the Community

The historical records on the Deaf community are littered with prescriptive and what now seem to be outrageous views on Deaf people. In this section, within a brief historical detour, we look at two controversial views as a way of identifying some preconceptions which professionals bring with them into their practice.

There are a number of conventional histories of deafness available[2] and, if you are interested in the historical aspect, it is worth reading these (though they are *not* essential reading for this course). They are largely concerned with the development of education, and the controversies which have existed in education right up to the present, about 'what is best for the deaf child'. There are few attempts to try to tell the Deaf story and these are rather doomed to failure since, in the past, the experiences of deafness were seldom written down. Perhaps one of the best attempts is that of Van Cleve and Crouch (1989) who examine the American Deaf community in the nineteenth century from the available records. There are attempts to gather Deaf writings or references to deafness (Batson and Bergman, 1976; Grant, 1987) but these are largely indicative of the hearing-enforced social view of the period in which the writings took place, since the writers, even the Deaf writers, are successes of the prevailing educational ethos. Interestingly, Van Cleve and Crouch (1989) point to the relative success of Thomas Gallaudet at the beginning of the nineteenth century in setting up the American School for the Deaf and laying the base for the development of Deaf higher education in the USA. Gallaudet's success contrasted with the failure of attempts by Thomas Braidwood, grandson of the original Braidwood who fathered the dynasty of oral-led schools for the deaf in the

[2] For example, Hodgson (1954), Lane (1984a,b), Scouten (1984) and McLoughlin (1987).

UK, to set up a model school in the USA at the same time. Gallaudet went for signing and opened the way for the development of a very different type of community in the USA.

The story of Deaf people cannot be told without reference to these hearing people: educators, welfare workers and others. The existence of Deaf people has often been despite the attempts of hearing people to ensure participation in this mainstream world and the attempt to ensure that Deaf people embraced this set of 'single-purpose communities'. Although we seek to understand the positive features of Deaf society, we must also be aware of its evolution in the face of often unspoken oppression. This may seem particularly harsh terminology, but largely misguided attempts to normalize Deaf people have caused untold hardships.

> Talk with even very worldly Deaf people educated in the old way and in more cases than not you will find surprisingly close to the surface and barely hidden by education, good manners, humour or experience, the running sores of anguish and resentment, the gaping, unstaunchable wounds of wrongs done decades before; a bottomless fury; an identical litany of slapped hands, tied wrists, punishments, scoldings, tedium, humiliation.
>
> (Benderly, 1980, p. 229)

These are apparently extreme and over-dramatic descriptions until one actually 'listens' to Deaf people.

> I had a lot of punishments for using my signings in classrooms and at playground. The teachers reported me to headmistress many times, then one morning at assembly I was caught again, then, ordered me to stand in front of the children, the headmistress announced that I looked like a monkey from the zoo, waving my hands everywhere. She thinks she will put me in a cage in the zoo so the people will laugh at a stupid boy in the cage.
>
> (Account by Deaf person in Kyle and Woll, 1985, p. 263)

> The deaf-mute, being without the power of speech, is debarred from entering by the usual means into communion with his fellow-men, and so loses one of the greatest charms of social life.
>
> (Scott, 1870, p. 56)

Many readers might point out that not much has changed in terms of expressed attitude in the UK. The point, of course, is that, in socializing, Deaf people were undervalued, ignored, discriminated against and at times actively vilified for their use of non-standard communication. The story of sign language will follow in Unit 3 and so will only be dealt with here in so far as it affects our consideration of community.

There are, however, two further historical aspects of great significance to our understanding. The first arises in the writings of Alexander Graham Bell and the second originates in the story of John Flournoy.

3.1 Alexander Graham Bell: a Deaf world

Bell is a classic model of a highly motivated, intelligent, technology-oriented professional working with Deaf people, married to a partially hearing wife, reacting to the unsatisfactory nature of Deaf education in a way which has proved extremely damaging to Deaf people everywhere. There is no doubt that Bell thought he was right in insisting that Deaf people could speak and ought to be integrated into society as a whole. He argued against sign language and was most violently opposed to the idea of Deaf people associating with and, in particular, marrying other Deaf people. His work influenced many professionals and he was one of a new breed of educators who proclaimed the takeover of deafness by oralism in the latter part of the nineteenth century. He contributed to the evidence in the 1889 Education Act in the UK as well as being a prolific writer in the USA.

Bell is important in the history of the Deaf community as a significant example of well-meaning hearing control which is ultimately oppressive. Despite his status in hearing society and despite the insight he had into the nature of deafness, he failed to understand the importance of the community which Deaf people had created. Ironically, in his paper on the creation of a Deaf variety of the human race, he sets out the steps required to create a separate Deaf culture. These are illuminating today as perhaps key markers of the Deaf community. In order to create a 'separate race' he suggested the following:

1 Separate children from their homes and gather them in large institutions.
2 Organize social clubs for adults after they leave school.
3 Give them their own newspapers and media.
4 Give them their own language and thought.
5 Reduce sign language to a written form.
6 Promulgate myths about Deaf people so that others avoid them.

Figure 2.2 Alexander Graham Bell, from a photograph taken in 1876 (Source: The Science Museum, London)

The clarity of this vision is impressive and it identifies the central aspects of what we can now proceed to call the 'Deaf community'. The features which are most obviously missing from Bell's conception are the commitment of the 'members' and the benefits accruing to members by dint of their membership. These are conspicuously overlooked in the pursuit of the 'pseudo-normalization' which denies deafness. Further, Bell adds that vital ingredient of oppression, control—as invested in power, dominance and decision-making. The very tone of Bell's suggestions are in keeping with the mistake consistently made by hearing educators, carers and professionals—that they have the power over Deaf people to determine the nature of their lives. The truth is simpler: while hearing society sets the institutional framework and service provision, Deaf people themselves construct and utilize the social dimension. The fact that hearing people have chosen to ignore this dimension does not make its impact less, it simply removes it from the public eye. The Deaf community has existed and will continue to exist beyond hearing people's perceptions if necessary, to meet the needs of Deaf people for identity and for social interchange. In this respect, Deaf people are no different from any other embattled minority group. However, this runs a little ahead of the discussion here. The importance of this hearing misunderstanding will be examined later in Sections 7 and 9.

3.2 John Flournoy: a Deaf homeland

However, there is one other part of the historical jigsaw which is of importance here. It is a significant concept in nearly every society and it has appeared at different times amongst Deaf people. It is the concept of a 'Deaf homeland'. It was first written about by John Flournoy in the 1850s, again by Jane Groom in the 1890s and has recently re-appeared in a novel called *Islay* by Douglas Bullard in 1986. The context for the first suggestion was the climate of the new world where religious intolerance had led various groups to stake out a piece of territory in the land where there seemed to be limitless natural resources.

John Flournoy, a Deaf man, frustrated in his attempts to seek positions within the government, wrote a circular letter to Deaf people in the USA and in Europe, setting out the idea of a Deaf state in the USA. The correspondence which this provoked in the American Annals of the Deaf is worth reading, though there is an excellent account in Van Cleeve and Crouch (1989). Flournoy's suggestion was for a state to be formed where all the power rested with Deaf people. Only Deaf people could determine the working of the society and hearing children would be allowed to leave when appropriate. Flournoy's mistake was probably to enter into a dialogue on the terms of the hearing decision-makers. He wrote to his old hearing teacher, William Turner, who was dismissive of the idea. The debate was then placed in the hands of the literate Deaf members of the New England Gallaudet Association. Laurent Clerc, at the age of 72, came out against the idea even though it was widely believed that he had suggested the idea in the first place some years before. Thomas Gallaudet, the son of the original Gallaudet, weighed in with what is always the most powerful blocking argument on Deaf rights—that the idea was 'not representative of the majority of Deaf people'. As has been common throughout Deaf history, such debates have been conducted by those deaf people most integrated into hearing society and as such the preferences of the Deaf people remain largely unexplored.

Jane Groom in the 1890s in England had rather more success in promoting the idea of independence for Deaf people and was able to obtain land and took Deaf people to Canada. This does not seem to have been an exclusively Deaf venture, however, and we know little of the final outcomes.

Groce (1985) reconstructs from historical sources a picture of a fully integrated Deaf–hearing society on Martha's Vineyard off the coast of New England. On the island the incidence of deafness was much higher than the average and Deaf and hearing people interacted freely using sign language and English. Although presented as an almost idyllic existence of mutual tolerance and effective communication, we have no direct evidence on the reality of this community and it is questionable if it could truly satisfy the need for Deaf people to have independence and self-determination.

◀ Reading
At this point, you should review the extract from Groce's book in Unit 1 and also read the longer extract which is reprinted as Article 1.2 'Everyone Here Spoke Sign Language', in Reader Two. ◀

The whole issue of a 'Deaf homeland' is a difficult and complex one. It strikes at the heart of the fears of any dominating majority and echoes the Pharaoh's fears when Moses announced that he was taking the Jews off to their promised land. It is doubly complex because Deaf people are usually born into hearing families and it is this argument which is most often presented to hearing parents as a stick with which to beat themselves—'if you are not attentive to your child's education you will lose him or her to the Deaf community'. The issues involved here are enormous. Because society has undervalued Deaf people in the past, it was seen by educators as vital that deaf children be trained for entry into hearing society. Deaf young people who preferred the company of other Deaf people were classed as failures. Now, we have a re-evaluation of Deaf people and have discovered the importance of Community life and the development of a Deaf identity. Deaf people themselves can now promote this aspect of their community. But one can see the dilemma for hearing parents who have been given these two conflicting messages.

Additionally, hearing parents have to cope with loss. At the beginning, it is the loss of the hearing child they wanted. Now it seems they might even lose the deaf child they have raised—to the Deaf community, of which the parents have never been part. Not surprisingly, adolescence can be a particularly difficult period for everyone concerned—the parents, the young person and the Deaf community. The problem may be seen as one of a family with mixed culture, but diagnosing or naming the difficulty does not make it any easier to handle. With a better understanding of Deaf people and the Community, right from the beginning, many of the points of conflict could be avoided or dealt with rather less stressfully. Ultimately, the problem can be solved only when there is mutual respect and understanding from both Deaf and hearing communities.

As you can see, we could probably have spent the whole of this unit looking at the sort of issues raised within the historical context. Although we may see these points of view and events as outdated and difficult to accept, they represent some aspects of the heritage of Deaf people, and are important in the same way that other cultural minorities draw on their historical roots to give meaning to their current existence.

4 The Deaf community: how to join and how to resign

As will now be becoming apparent to you, the Deaf community, growing in adversity, is not a single society with one purpose which one can 'sign up for'. It is a diverse meeting of individuals who come together for many purposes but who share some basics of experience, communication and commitment. There has been discussion in the past on the extent of the Deaf community, and it has become clear that it is not helpful to try to define the Deaf community in terms of pathology. The medical/educational definitions of loss and lack of abilities do not describe the nature of the Community adequately. The simplest and one of the most effective definitions is provided by Baker and Padden (1978).

> The deaf community comprises those deaf and hard-of-hearing individuals who share a common language, common experiences and values and a common way of interacting with each other and with hearing people. The most basic factor determining who is a member of the deaf community seems to be what is called 'attitudinal deafness'. This occurs when a person identifies him/herself as a member of the deaf community and other members accept that person as part of the community.

> (Baker and Padden, 1978, p. 4)

In this section I will be concerned most with central members of the Community and will not enter into discussion of sub-groups within the Community or those groups which are marginal or have a complicated relationship with the Community. Groups such as black deaf people, gay deaf people, deaf-blind people and oral deaf people will be included in Unit 4.

4.1 How to join

Some people are 'born into' the Deaf community in an obvious way as the children of Deaf parents. These are the minority since only 5 to 6 per cent of children in schools for the deaf will have both parents Deaf, and up to a further 5 per cent may have one parent Deaf (based on Conrad, 1979. This is possibly the most reliable figure since it includes most deaf schoolchildren of a particular age group. It is likely that the percentage is higher among those people who attend a Deaf club—hence, Jackson's (1986) figure of 10.9 per cent. Some care must be taken with these figures). Up to 20 per cent will have a deaf sibling. Other Deaf members are drawn from families where there is no deafness and where there is a likelihood of isolation as an early experience. Whilst it is difficult to know how many Deaf people come from Deaf families, it is even more difficult to predict how many are likely to have sign language from an early age. Where parents are hearing-impaired there can be no simple assumption that sign language is used. Because of beliefs about the limitation of signing, which parents have experienced in their development, they may be anxious that their children grow up differently and 'more successfully' in English. This may lead them to try to use English even with their deaf children. This is not an uncommon situation for language minorities. For most children with some early contact with the Community, the issue of communication will be rather straightforward—sign language will be acquired and used in all situations where effective interaction is required. For those with no contact with other Deaf people in the early years, the communication problems can be immense. In our work on deaf children in hearing families (Kyle and Ackerman, in preparation) and in reported work (Gregory and Barlow, 1989) there are major difficulties for the deaf child in a hearing-only environment.

These problems may take the form of unresolved identity and mistaken beliefs about adulthood:

> When did I realize I was deaf?
>
> I was nine or ten when I first went to a Deaf club. That was the first time that I realized that adults could be deaf, that it was not just children. When I was very young I had thought everybody was deaf, but as I grew older I realized it was not everybody, but then I thought it was only children. Then when I saw those deaf adults I realized that they could be deaf too—and that was when I realized that I would grow up to be a deaf adult.
>
> (24-year-old deaf woman—glossed from an interview in British Sign Language)

> Yes, even now I think that I might wake up and my hearing will be perfect, and I would speak better. Whether I would feel better or be happier I don't know. Certainly, when I was little I believed that one day I would hear.
>
> (20-year-old deaf man—from an interview in spoken English)

> I was in the second year at Mary Hare School. I'd never met deaf adults then, and I said to my mum that when I grew up I would be hearing. After all, all the teachers were hearing. I was upset when she told me I'd always be deaf. Then I was worried that I'd be the only one, that there would be no other deaf adults.
>
> (21-year-old man, from notes taken at an interview conducted in spoken English)
>
> (From work in progress: S. Gregory, J. Bishop and L. Sheldon)

Such problems mean that for the majority of the Deaf community fluency in the core language may come later than is usual for the acquisition of spoken languages, and it also means that the early experiences of childhood which those Community members have, will be unsatisfactory ones in relation to the struggle for meaning and for interaction.

Experience as a marker is obvious when one considers Bell's set of principles for the creation of the Community. Deaf people have peer interaction at school as a central positive experience of Community life. Contact with hearing people at school is often painful and may produce a deep resentment which is either directed inwardly as a devaluation of one's own abilities ('I am Deaf and therefore no good—I can't …') or else becomes a 'rebellious nature' which produces a school history of frustration and aggression (when young) and of punishments and behaviour problems. Unfortunately, perhaps, it is mostly the former response which is created and which leaves the Deaf adolescent as accepting of the 'disabling' socialization. These adolescents believe that 'deaf means can't'. A gradual re-awakening of belief in the Community over the last few years has led to a shaking off of this image amongst the Deaf leadership in the UK and to a reassertion of the positive aspects of early life and with it a rejection of the priorities of hearing educators.

British Sign Language (BSL), which will be described in Unit 3, is acquired in childhood. Even those in hearing families claim to have learned the language before the age of 12 years and where we have more detailed records on the school history, Kyle and Pullen (1985) found that 90 per cent of profoundly deaf young people had learned sign by the age of 12 years and 48 per cent of partially hearing people had learned while at school. Despite the fact that BSL was not tolerated by educators in the school lives of most of the young people interviewed by Kyle and Pullen, they claim to have learned and used it while still at school. It becomes clear that signing is a key part of deaf children's interaction.

When Kyle and Allsop (1982) asked 175 Deaf people about what constituted Community membership, there was strong evidence that Deaf people saw membership in terms of making a commitment and displaying the desire to associate with other Deaf people. All the statements relating to the inabilities of Deaf people were rejected firmly. Although the Deaf club was not absolutely vital to Community membership, it was absolutely vital to Community life. Of the population interviewed, 58 per cent attended the Deaf club once a week or more, though a sizeable group (29 per cent) went to the Deaf club very rarely. Those who did go were reckoned to be 'proud to be Deaf' (81 per cent), because they liked other Deaf people's company (97 per cent) or because they were treated as normal there (97 per cent). When asked about who could be members of the Community, it was possible for those who became deaf to join (74 per cent agreed), and even for those who did not sign (70 per cent) but there was no place for those whose identification was with hearing people or those who had been to hearing school. What is clear is that primary identification with the Deaf community is the key.

In a sample of 421 Deaf people, Jackson (1986) reported similar findings—that the attitudinal dimension is central to the issue of membership. In addition, he confirmed the multi-faceted side of the Community when very few respondents suggested that they attended the Deaf club just for single specific activities. The nature of the Deaf community is, therefore, very different from the single-purpose worlds which hearing people join.

In terms of the question of how to join the Community, it begins to be clear that the main factor is the desire to associate with other Deaf people; this in turn is related to the sharing of experiences in childhood and adolescence and is centred on deafness itself and on the use of sign language.

20

To refer back to the discussion at the beginning of this section, the ease with which people 'join' is directly related to whether they have Deaf parents themselves. In a study of children, Harris and Stirling (1986) found that those with Deaf parents were much more certain of their Deaf identity and tended to predict their status as Deaf adults. Those from hearing families were more likely to believe that they would become hearing or hard-of-hearing and were more likely to have internalized the educators' (and their parents') goals of speech and involvement in the hearing society. At the point where Community membership is considered by these young people, they begin to talk of 'coming to terms with their deafness', but it usually comes at the end of a long struggle both with themselves and with others in hearing settings. Robinson (1989), educated in an oral framework and in integrated schools, describes her first steps:

> It was when I started sixth form college and made friends with another Deaf girl that I finally began to learn to accept my Deafness. I began to go to classes in BSL with my mum and my sister. Through the teacher I began to understand Deaf culture. Recently I went to a Deaf Club. I was really at ease and felt that I did not have to put on a front as with hearing people. It's helped me to gain confidence …

> Always having been in hearing schools I have never actually belonged to the Deaf community. Now I want to discover my roots by finding out more about what it means to me to be Deaf and how it affects other people.
>
> (Robinson, 1989, p. 7)

In this discovery Robinson is not alone—Lawson (1981) has described people like Robinson as the 'late-comers' to the Community. Young (1989), in his response to the statement by Robinson, illustrates how pleased the Deaf community is when Deaf people begin to discover their identity:

> I congratulate Joanne on her victory. She has become part of the Deaf community with its own language, values and heritage. The pride and confidence which she now feels is an important element in the struggle which Deaf people face in gaining equality.
>
> (Young, 1989, p. 7)

The discussion so far has concentrated on the issue of personal identity as 'the way into' the Community. However, some Deaf people report that even where there is a desire to join or to be part of the Community, other members reject them. The basis for this rejection is difficult to pin down precisely: there are some people who do not fit in because of previous contacts with members of that group, or there may be a history of resentment or a lack of understanding of someone who has come to deafness by a different route—those who lose their hearing would be a good example. Some people rejected in one Deaf club may find themselves accepted elsewhere. These factors are common to any established group or society. No one person decides on who can be a member, nor is there a rational reason for acceptance or rejection in many cases. The features described as key markers (language, attitude, identity) remain central but other personal and inter-personal aspects may intrude. It is important also to note that people living in isolated parts of the country would still be considered as part of the Community even if they are very rarely seen by others.

◄ Activity 6

It would be helpful to pause for a moment and consider the communities of which you are member and to think about your first tentative steps to 'join'. How did you feel about your likely acceptance? Contrast this with returning to your most comfortable social group where you do have your strongest identity. You should be aware of the ease of fitting into a group where you do not have to negotiate all the interaction and where there are others with similar ideas and experiences. ◄

4.2 How to resign

In Section 4.1 it became clear that involvement in the Deaf community required a degree of commitment to the Community as a whole—you can't join just for the bingo—and that this decision is tied up in the resolution of the identity problem. It then becomes obvious that one cannot resign simply by non-attendance, there has to be a realignment of loyalties. For most Deaf people such a realignment of loyalties is unlikely—it would be very difficult to switch off the Deaf part and identify more with hearing people. There are situations where this is possible to some extent—a mixed marriage is an example where a Deaf person may feel more drawn to the hearing society of the spouse and may forsake Deaf company—nevertheless, it is unlikely that the person's identity as a Deaf person changes.

Perhaps the most difficult situations occur when an individual breaks the rules of the Community in some way. These can be directly in the case of Deaf club rules which often carry penalties such as life-time bans, or less directly when the individual offends against the social norms. In these circumstances, the individual may find himself or herself ostracized by the others. One of the more difficult instances of this is in the case of divorce within the Community. Because the numbers of Deaf people in any one area of the country tend to be small, marital break-ups, particularly where there is infidelity, are likely to be public knowledge and it is then likely that one party will find it difficult to face the other members of the Community. A period of isolation is likely to follow when contact with friends is painful or non-existent.

Attendance at Deaf clubs may be declining on account of the other attractions of home life, such as subtitled television and the use of Minicoms to keep in contact by telephone, but these reductions in face-to-face contact do not constitute resignation from the Community. While Baker and Cokely (1980) felt that the American Deaf clubs were declining in importance, the Community is still alive.

Because involvement in the Deaf community is part of an identity resolution, it has a different status to that of hearing 'communities' and as such it is very difficult to opt out, once in. To attempt to do so is to create another identity crisis and this in itself can be problematic.

5 The Deaf community and its characteristics

In the next two sections we will examine those areas of the Community about which we seem to know most. These are the well-researched but rather superficial areas of socio-economic activity and education, and we have to probe quite deeply into them to contribute significantly to our picture of the Community. Schein and Delk (1974) have carried out the largest study to date in their census of the American deaf population, Jackson's (1986) study in the UK provides a very good indication of the issues, and Kyle and Woll (1985) summarize some of the key points of earlier studies in Britain.

5.1 Employment

The most common observation on employment is that deaf people are 'under-employed rather than unemployed'. Kyle and Allsop (1982) report unemployment of 8.6 per cent, and Kyle and Pullen (1985) of 15 per cent (among 23-year-olds)—general adult unemployment in the UK varies from 8 per cent to 15 per cent. In terms of type of job, all studies confirm the under-employment. Deaf people generally have jobs in the unskilled and semi-skilled occupations (62 per cent as compared to around 25 per cent of hearing people: Kyle and Pullen, 1985). Generally less than 3 per cent are found in Social Class 1 (Professional/Managerial), though this is also a less common category for hearing people. Kyle and Allsop (1982) found that very few Deaf people ever reached a position of supervision over others and the prospects for promotion were very bleak for most.

Kyle and Woll (1985) report that Deaf people were generally happy at work even given the fact that very few had another Deaf person in the same factory or division. Nevertheless, the statistics tend to hide the great gulf in the quality of working life between Deaf and hearing people. Foster (1986), in an examination of graduates of the National Technical Institute for the Deaf in the USA, found many areas of problems when she interviewed Deaf workers. Although all felt competent in the carrying out of their job, communication difficulties were often a major barrier. Most of the workers were lonely at work, spending most of their free time on their own. Their career goals tended to be lowered after initial contact with the workplace—supervisory roles were usually ruled out. Over half described situations in which they felt they had been treated unfairly.

This rather bleak picture is also reflected in the report of the Royal National Institute for the Deaf (RNID), *Communication Works: Inquiry into the Employment of Deaf People* (RNID, 1988) which was designed to illustrate some of the problems. As well as setting out the same issues as above, they used some case studies:

> FF began work and it was soon apparent that her skills—particularly in literacy and language—were much less developed than had been realised. The expectations that she would pass through the training course rapidly and would soon be a productive member of the team were found to be unrealistic. This had several consequences.

Firstly, it put FF under a lot of strain. She felt she was not succeeding in her job. Secondly, the co-worker assigned to FF was having to try to do her ordinary work as well as helping FF to do hers—this produced great stress. Thirdly, the planning department found itself effectively short-staffed and began to experience delays in processing applications. Again, there was increased stress throughout. Finally the relationship between hearing staff, the sign language interpreter and the deaf worker began to deteriorate.

(RNID, 1988, p. 21)

Although these negative experiences at the interface with the hearing community are not untypical, and though they are significant ones for Deaf people in the conduct of their lives, it should be pointed out that the *major* problems are in the transition phases between jobs or from school to work. It is at these points that expectations may be greatest on the part of both hearing and Deaf workers and when the greatest difficulties arise.

Schein (1987) confirms most of the employment results for deaf people from all walks of life in the USA. Stinson (1970) suggests that under-employment arises because of poor self-image, though given the problems of stress and pressure from hearing society, the low self-esteem is likely to be a product rather than a cause. Christiansen (1982) attributes the under-employment of Deaf people to the change in the economy from a base in manufacturing to a base in service industry. Deaf people are simply not represented well in services. He concludes:

In general, it appears that in order to secure a given job in the labour force, a deaf person must be better educated, and more qualified, than a hearing person vying for the same position.

(Christiansen, 1982, p. 19)

Significantly, there are also differences between white and non-white Deaf people in employment. Non-white Deaf people are less likely to be employed and are likely to earn much less.

Jones and Pullen (1987), in the first part of a major study of Deaf people in Europe, broadly confirm these findings in the perception of Deaf people. They found evidence of under-employment, thwarted ambition and even occupational segregation, attributed to the type of expectancies built up by schooling. Interestingly, they found that jobs were usually acquired through personal contacts rather than on the open market or through the rehabilitation or job-finding agencies. This might be a factor in Deaf people becoming 'stuck' in one level of employment as it is difficult to see how their employment needs could have been adequately evaluated in that situation.

The picture of employment is therefore not a happy one in many respects and constitutes a great waste of potential. (Remember that hearing loss does not produce a decrease in intellectual capacity, and so Deaf people will be just as cognitively competent as hearing people.) The reasons for such problems would normally be considered to lie in the education Deaf people receive, and most investigators have considered this a major factor.

5.2 Education

All the major studies of national groups in different countries highlight educational failure on a massive scale. Although education will be dealt with more extensively in Unit 5, it is important to consider it here in relation to understanding the Community in order to build up some picture of the likely outcomes of deaf children's education. Deaf children read poorly (profoundly deaf 16-year-olds at an average reading age of less than 9 years), speak unintelligibly and have limited lip-reading skills (Conrad, 1979). They are less likely to go to college in the USA (Christiansen, 1982), though more likely to go into further education in the UK (Kyle and Pullen, 1985).

The purpose here is not to highlight these failures—which in any case can be compared to other minority groups in the UK—but rather to consider the impact that such a situation has on the Deaf community itself. The effect is colossal. On the one hand, the schooling often produces great feelings of failure either during schooldays or when entering the work-place, and on the other, the schooling itself is disabling when it institutionalizes deafness (in large residential settings) and when it represses the formation of a successful identity. In many respects, Deaf young people may leave school pre-programmed to fail and to accept the failure. They move from childhood into a powerless situation in adult life—often being found a job by their school or by parents, and left at the lower levels of the salary structure. Even when the possibilities for pressure towards change occur, Deaf people are unable to take up the challenge because of their learned helplessness.

One 'obvious' solution to this problem is to avoid the separateness of the deaf school by mainstreaming the deaf child from the earliest age, and thus avoiding the perils mentioned above. Unfortunately, unlike some 'disabled' groups, this may not be a solution for Deaf people. However, before going on to see why this might be so, it is important to note that there are two levels to the effect of deaf schooling. On the one hand, we can see the negative acceptance of failure in society at large as it develops in the child and young adult, but on the other there is the tremendous advantage of the creation of identity. While schooling may be a disarming experience on one level, it is a crucially important one on the other level. Through the continuing contact with other Deaf people (even where there are no adult role models), language and culture grow. The key adolescent stage of establishing identity is met in a community environment where confidence in communication and social interaction can be experienced. For many Deaf young people this could be the most important period of their lives, when the socialization takes place not from adult models but from other Deaf young people. It is not surprising, therefore, that one of the first questions that Deaf people ask each other on meeting is which school the other attended.

Mainstreaming has become one of the most controversial issues for Deaf people and one which mixes the desired promise of acceptance by and equal status with hearing people, with the stark reality of constant difference and the enormity of the language gap. Integration procedures have existed in deaf education since just after the Second World War and it has always been the case that a majority of *hearing-impaired* children are in ordinary schools. The proportion of *Deaf* children is difficult to determine since it is possible to utilize the statistics of hearing loss in many different ways, but it can be seen that many Deaf young people no longer have the experience of schooling in direct contact with other Deaf children.

This trend is now widespread across the UK. For many groups, special education had been an isolating and frustrating experience; for physically handicapped young people in particular, the effects of their separate schooling had been to disable them in the able-bodied world. Integration offered the possibility of closer contact and thereby greater likelihood of acceptance and success. For parents, the attractions of having their children treated as equals in an ordinary school are just too great. Linked to this is the finding in Conrad's study of deaf school-leavers that there are no measurable differences in academic achievement between special school children and integrated children (when one controls degree of hearing loss) (Conrad, 1979). Unfortunately, when we look at the observational research on deaf children we find that the outcomes in the classroom in the mainstream are not good.

Gregory and Bishop (1989), in a language and interaction study of deaf children in ordinary schools, found that the quality of interaction was greatly impaired and that the language actually accessible to the deaf child was considerably less than was available to the hearing classmates.

◄ Reading
This article, 'The Mainstreaming of Primary Age Deaf Children' by Susan Gregory and Juliet Bishop, is Article 5.11 in Reader Two and you should read this now.

You may also find Article 5.10, 'Challenging Conceptions of Integration' by Tony Booth, in Reader Two helpful in this debate. ◄

However, one of the most direct criticisms of integration comes from Ladd (1981) who was mainstreamed during his education. It is worth detailing his insights of the boy in a mainstream school (there is an updated version of this paper in Reader One, Article 10 'Making plans for Nigel: the Erosion of Identity by Mainstreaming', which you might like to look at):

> He survives by cunning; his homework is copied or else is simple enough to pick up from the textbook alone. He does poorly in term time but better in exams; the strain forces him to specialise and he is literally top in a couple of subjects and bottom in others. He understands few of the events that the school involves itself in; it is impossible for him to hear in meetings and he develops a terror of drama, gym, science and art where you have to demonstrate whether you have understood by carrying things out.
>
> (Ladd, 1981, pp. 408–9)

It is easy to see how the illusion of success is possible to maintain for a deaf child in such a setting. Deaf children are unlikely to be a behavioural problem (or they would have been moved), and since the currency of integration is whether the child 'seems to have settled or appears to be coping', there is very little actual monitoring of the cognitive and psychological development of the child. The pressures on the child are immense.

All this has an effect on him, and at home he stays in more and more, inventing and playing games alone. As close to the womb as he can get. I must be careful not to paint things too black. They *are* that black, but when you are growing up you don't know any different; you are told repeatedly that this is what growing up to be a man is all about. You still hate it, but because of this, it rules out suicide as an option.

(Ibid., p. 410)

These are harsh words—all the more so as they come in a situation where this person has been surrounded by well-meaning adults. It is also striking that the young person does not know 'any different'. The effects of the integration remain unevaluated. But the effects begin to be apparent in the search for an identity in adolescence.

His search for an identity becomes more intense. 'I'm an introvert, that's it. I can't follow things. But that's not because I'm deaf. They told me I wasn't deaf, just that I can't hear very well. So if I can't follow, it must be because I'm thick. That must be true. I can never think of anything to talk about to others except football. So that's what I am.' Now he is truly split in half. His rational mind says that he can't be thick because he is where he is, whilst his emotional mind sees no other alternative identity.

Oh Ewing, Oh Van Uden, what a marvellous choice you gave us deaf children! To see ourselves as stupid rather than to be able to see ourselves as deaf and accept it and work from there.

(Ibid., p. 411)

Such views are not untypical, though clearly there are others who never reach the stage of comprehension that Ladd has reached and so continue to believe in their success. There are others who reach Ladd's conclusions but have no means of expressing themselves adequately and their lives end in suicide. There are no figures for such problems in the world of Deaf people but nearly every Deaf person whom one could approach could list a number of others who have found the identity problem and frustration too much.

 ◀ Activity 7
The issues of identity and membership of a community are very difficult to imagine if you have never found yourself in a situation where your self-esteem was called into question. Few of us on courses ever really fail. Try to recall visits you might have made to a foreign country when you have been on your own and surrounded by speakers of another language—where you are quite clearly the foreigner. List the feelings you had at the time and consider how easy it was for you to ask questions or obtain answers. ◀

◀ Comment
What you may have found is that, first, it is difficult to remember any situation in which you were completely a 'foreigner'—we avoid those situations as far as possible because we have an inherent fear of this isolation. When it does happen we usually feel unable to ask questions and also very uncertain of the responses. The solution is to ask safe questions to which we can predict the answers. This is the situation in which many Deaf people find themselves for much of the time. ◀

Education and employment are two areas where we seem to have a great deal in the way of statistics but little insight. Both create experiences which shape the lives of Deaf people and thereby have an impact on the Community. Up to now, hearing people have been satisfied with assurances from each other that the statistics were fine, or, if they were not (as in the case of reading problems), then they were a direct result of the deafness. Rarely have we taken note of the views of Deaf people or paused to look behind the statistical and audiological entity to try to understand the experience of deafness.

◀ Activity 8

Examine two of the communities you noted in Activity 4 in Section 2, of which you are a member. Describe the characteristics of the members in terms of the dimensions we have highlighted for Deaf people—educational background and employment. Consider how important these factors have been in determining the power of the community in which you are involved. ◀

◀ Comment

What you may find, as in the case of Deaf people, is that there is a range of ability and background but the likelihood is that the power of the group to raise money, to influence others, to determine its own future, is directly related to the status of the members. For Deaf people the effects of education and the consequent poorer jobs obtained are a major problem in improving their situation. ◀

6 The Deaf community as a social structure

As in education, two different levels of activity in the Deaf community have been developed. On one level we have provision and associations. On the other level we have Deaf people, their interaction and what an experienced social worker once described as 'their secret language'.

Throughout the UK there is a network of Deaf clubs and societies. Most have their origins in the associations initiated by Deaf people but organized by hearing missioners. Some remain as charitable bodies with their own Trust Deed and Trustees or Board of Hearing Management. Some are still dominated by the Church. In the nineteenth century, these associations catered for the moral and spiritual welfare of Deaf people as well as providing further education and often providing training in a trade. Many were stifling of initiative, being wholly controlled by hearing people who could sign and could function well in the hearing world. They offered an infrastructure which allowed Deaf people to interact and they provided a meeting place. Modern day social work and attitudes towards charity and care have changed these voluntary organizations to a great extent. Nevertheless, in order to find out about deafness it is still the most natural thing to ask the principal of the club or the senior social worker.

This infrastructure is seldom part of the 'Deaf way' (a term discussed later in Section 9.4). The major interaction among Deaf people takes place on a different plane which only occasionally interfaces with this organization.

Deaf clubs rise and fall in popularity over seemingly short periods of time, often to the complete bewilderment of the hearing officers. The social club can be seen as the heart of Community life, though it would be wrong to see it as the only locus of that life. Nevertheless, it is the one area with which hearing people have had very little contact and on which the pressures of the hearing society are least obvious.

From the social club Deaf people organize activities, care for the children and for elderly people, arrange trips, create inter-club events. This is the forum for interaction. This is where the language is most effective. This is the source of Deaf culture. Here we find a regular focus for adults and children (both Deaf and hearing) and the opportunity to meet new people, to court and to marry. For inter-club activities, Deaf young people may travel 40 or 50 miles to a disco or social gathering. Regional rallies also draw large numbers.

The larger the membership of the club the wider the range of activities (both sports and social) and the greater the degree of social skill required. As a result, the social organization becomes more pronounced in such clubs. The skills of the Deaf management become greater and the value of the club as a resource to marginal Deaf people increases. In most clubs Deaf members will contribute something in kind to the development—possibly by making or fixing the fabric of the building or perhaps by regular provision of services. In return, the club is the place where the language conflicts dissolve and the experiences of employment and education can be put into perspective.[3]

Jackson (1986) spends a great part of his study examining the role of the Deaf club. He places the opportunity to socialize with other Deaf people as the principal reason for going to the club (72 per cent of responses). This was perceived as the main reason for others' involvement and Jackson confirms that the attendance pattern was one of a multi-faceted locus rather than of a single-purpose association. Interestingly, almost half of the membership were satisfied with their leadership and half were not. Satisfaction went with the perception that the leadership was hard-working and did its best for the club. Dissatisfaction went with characteristic views such as members of the leadership being too secretive, or not mixing, or being in it only for themselves.

In many respects, the Deaf club functions as the 'heart of the village of Deaf people' but the Community is more than the village community, requiring commitment, shared identity and mutual respect.

◀ Video
At this point you should pause in your reading of this section and review Video One, *Sandra's Story: The History of a Deaf Family*, paying particular attention to the sequence at the Deaf Club.◀

---

[3] Higgins (1980a) gives a good description of this aspect of Deaf life in the USA, and Kyle and Allsop (1982) have described features of it in Britain.

◄ Reading
You should now read for yourself about the Deaf community in Reader Two:

Article 2.1, 'Outsiders in a Hearing World' by Paul Higgins;
Article 2.3, 'The Modern Deaf Community' by Paddy Ladd;
Article 2.4, 'The Deaf Community and the Culture of Deaf People' by Carol Padden.

And also in the Set Book by Kyle and Woll, *Sign Language: The Study of Deaf People and Their Language*, Chapter 1.

This should help clarify some of the features of the Deaf community and allow you to offer a set of descriptors for the members of the Deaf community. ◄

7 Hearing people

Kyle and Allsop (1982) and Jackson (1986) point out that there is a place for hearing people in the Deaf club. The question of whether hearing people belong in the Deaf community is rather more difficult to answer. People with a hearing *attitude* are generally excluded. There is not space here to go into detail about various roles and experiences, but some of the features of the different hearing groups who have contact with the Deaf community (teachers, interpreters, parents) are set out by Kyle and Woll (1985), and Higgins (1980a) offers further insight. However, some mention should be made of the position of social workers in relation to the Deaf community. George Firth in his book *Chosen Vessels* presents a fascinating description of the missioners, social workers, chaplains and community workers with Deaf people over the years (Firth, 1989). While tending to list the personal history of the individual, the book also offers some insights into the way in which the work was viewed as a mission rather than as a service, demanding full commitment and often continuing presence in the Deaf club.

No matter how we see the purpose of social work in relation to the Community, there are many pitfalls. The first area of danger is British Sign Language, or rather the lack of it. It would be less than satisfactory to have workers with the Urdu-speaking minority who were unable to converse easily and freely with their 'clients'. It would be very difficult to deal with any crisis in such a group if the social worker did not have an extensive grasp of the cultural differences. Yet when it comes to the area of deafness the prevailing mythology is often derived from the medical–pathological model—that is, the 'problems of deafness' are tied up in the Deaf person's lack of English, and the confusions or difficulties which occur in social work practice arise as a result of the Deaf person's inability to communicate in English speech. When a social worker comes from the English majority, there is little pressure from within the service to acquire BSL.

There is an acknowledgement that 'signing' is important but this has been, and still is, focused on a form of signing which simply supports the spoken English. When it comes to emotional, difficult or threatening issues, the communication mode of the hearing person reverts to English speech with a few signs thrown in where they are known. Unfortunately, when we analyse such communication from a Deaf person's point of view, we find huge omissions in the signed part of the message (even though the corresponding words were spoken) and what is left is so dominated by English that it requires the Deaf person to have extensive skills in English in order to translate from the presented message into something which can be understood. Although this is a rather bleak diagnosis, it is supported by the evidence collected on 130 Social Workers with Deaf People (Kyle *et al.*, 1981), and although there has been a great increase in sign courses in the UK, there is still some way to go before we solve this problem.

From the point of view of Deaf people, the major consideration is whether the social worker can sign and it is not wise to assume that a new social worker can learn 'on the job'. Attempting to acquire the language when one is under pressure to understand a critical message from a Deaf person in distress is simply not feasible. As the number of repetitions of the message are increased to overcome the communication problem, the whole credibility of the social worker dissolves. There are few situations in which we can hold to the view that this only 'requires a low level of BSL skill'; in reality, BSL is necessary in every case at least as a resource and as a way of ensuring the confidence of the social worker. Competence at an advanced level of BSL use is essential for working in this field. (CACDP[4] stage 2 should be a starting point.)

It is possible to argue that in the social work field there is a concern for all aspects of deafness (from partial hearing loss to acquired hearing loss in old age), that there is much to do in the area of Deaf people with additional problems (physical, behavioural), that there is a complex area of mental health and adjustment to consider, and that social workers are also concerned with environmental aids and links to other support services. From this point of view, one can claim that work with the Deaf community is infrequent (since the social work base is distant from the Deaf club). Nevertheless, from the point of view of those who are Deaf, any contact requires that the professional is sensitive to the language and cultural differences. It has to be seen as a very high priority.

Other pitfalls for hearing workers are those of being drawn into interpreting situations. In all areas of language there are instances where someone with a basic knowledge is called upon to interpret in an informal setting, to facilitate information exchange. Such exchange is vital and there may be no interpreters in the vicinity. A social worker's skills may be confidently shared. However, the mode of exchange should be consecutive—the first person speaks/signs, then the facilitator speaks/signs, then the second person responds and so on. Simultaneous interpreting in any context is a very high level skill which requires a great deal of training and experience before it can be done properly—it should be avoided unless such training has been completed.

◀ Activity 9
These points give some general idea of the issues to be faced by hearing people in contact with the Deaf community. As someone with a direct interest in this process, you may find it useful at this stage to itemize the concerns you might have if you were to become involved with members of the Deaf community, or to list the factors you have already discovered as problematic if you are already involved in the Community. By considering your own communities and the membership problems that people can face, try to work out solutions to those concerns you have listed. ◀

[4] CACDP—Council for the Advancement of Communication with Deaf People—offers curricula and assessment in signing at three levels. It is increasingly recognized as offering the principal route to signing competence.

A more serious problem arises because of the present lack of trained interpreters. Social workers may be the only people with enough of a grasp of BSL to act as facilitators. This role should be invoked very rarely and with great care. It should be made clear to all parties that the social worker is 'acting as an interpreter' and that it may be necessary to clarify points during the process. The biggest difficulty in this situation is that the social worker is usually a member of the hearing majority and so cultural identification will be with the hearing/speakers in the exchange. As a result, the Deaf person gets the worst of the deal when the intermediary is untrained.

There are many other areas of social work practice not mentioned here which will be covered in later units. The major message about social work practice in this unit is that the twin concerns of language use and knowledge of culture are at times as much criticized in Social Workers with Deaf People as they are in educators. There is a danger that, because of the pressures of the job and the weight of the bureaucracy surrounding social work practice, the issues are never resolved even by those social workers with years of experience. Contact with established social work practice may reinforce old attitudes about community and language unless the more recent perspectives can be adopted. Improvement of this situation must be a high priority.

8 The non-deaf community

As has become apparent, those who are born Deaf into Deaf families are the core of the Deaf community, having had a direct transmission of BSL and cultural values. Other people with a hearing loss vary in their distance from the centre of the Community. Those with a severe or profound hearing loss from birth, who have attended schools for the deaf but who were born into hearing families, are natural members and form the majority of the membership. Partially hearing people whose loss has meant some degree of special education will have a place in the Community but may or may not take it up as they choose to learn and use BSL. A common link to the Community for a partially hearing person is through marriage to a Community member. Partially hearing young people are often drawn to the fringes of the Community at discos and other social gatherings. Occasionally, 'young hard-of-hearing clubs' are seen within the Deaf club. In these instances, there is some degree of interaction with members of the Community and a nominal membership for the partially hearing people themselves.

Two large groups stand out as hearing-impaired, however, who have very little to do with the Community, yet who may form their own association. These are people who lose their hearing either during their careers or around or after retirement.

Kyle and Wood (1983) interviewed around 100 people who had lost their hearing during their working lives, and Jones et al. (1987) worked with another 130 families with members between the ages of 20 and 60 years, who had lost their hearing. The finding of the first study was that there was no 'community' of people with an acquired loss. For them the identification

32

was with other hearing people and no desire to associate specifically with others who had experienced a loss was found. This is predictable in that it is no easier to lip-read a person who has a hearing loss than it is to lip-read one without. Subsequent to this finding, the National Association of Deafened People (NADP) was formed to meet the needs of exactly this group of people. At the same time, the USA saw the colossal growth of the hard-of-hearing organization Self Help for the Hard-of-Hearing (SHHH). The rationale behind the growth of SHHH was that people with an acquired loss had much to share and that learning and adjustment could come about through this contact with one another. A similar feeling of empathy can be seen in the papers from the conference on 'Adjustment to Acquired Hearing Loss' (Kyle, 1987) in which presenters wanted to share their experiences in a productive way (Woolley, 1987—Article 31 in Reader One; Hase, 1987). NADP in the UK has tended not to function in this way and remains at an early stage of development in terms of establishing its policies and practices.

These moves caused some re-evaluation of the position that those with acquired hearing loss do not form a community. But in the light of the study of families (Jones *et al.*, 1987), it is still accurate to maintain that those with an acquired loss continue to retain their 'cultural hearingness' and are unlikely to shift their identity. As a result, in the UK at least, associations for the deafened are largely single-purpose societies which require a different level of commitment from their membership. Just as with the hearing population, the members will have involvement in many other clubs and societies and be able to pass from 'world to world' even though the transitions may not be as easy as they would be for those with perfect hearing.

Those acquiring hearing loss late in life fall into a different category since they may have less pressure on them to adjust and yet may meet with antagonism because of their failure to change to suit the younger members of society around them. They are frequently the butt of jokes and it is apparently 'socially acceptable' to tease and even insult such people in company. Few studies of this particular group have been carried out in the UK and most of those that have been done are concerned with whether or not such people can be prevailed upon to wear their hearing aids.

There have been no studies of social concerns in relation to this group— however, SHHH in the USA encompasses many older people and it is clear that they do not fit the stereotype of elderly hard-of-hearing who frequent senior citizen clubs where communication is interrupted by frequent calls for repetition. At present, it is not possible to designate such a group as a community, but they represent an ever-increasing population and will require much more attention and research from social services.

9 Deaf cultural life

By this point it should be clear what the thrust of the argument is. Deaf people are unique because of their hearing loss, early experiences, language and community commitment. In many respects they function like a minority group. Almost certainly they have a firm base of 'culture'. Previous definitions of the pathology of deafness do not predict membership of the

Deaf community and are misleading for any serious student of this Community. The history of pressures to 'abolish deafness' and to 'normalize' through oral language, have meant that the emergence of Deaf ethnicity has been painful and characterized by both overt and covert oppression. Not surprisingly, cultural life has been hidden from prying eyes. It has been greatly suppressed as lack of confidence in language has taken away the confidence for public performance. This has begun to change very recently because of the media interest in BSL and the awareness of its place among the 'visual arts'. 'High culture', as this form of public performance may be termed, is increasingly apparent in Deaf poetry festivals and drama productions.

 ◀ Video
Dorothy Miles can be seen on Video Two (Sequence Six) signing a poem. You should examine this at some length to gauge the rhythmic and spatial aspects of the performance as well as trying to understand its meaning. Poetry of this sort is a prized skill and one which remains relatively uncommon. ◀

The position of translated theatre (where an interpreter is present) or where sign and voice are used by the actors (as in the play *Children of a Lesser God* by Mark Medoff) is ambiguous. Deaf people may choose not to attend as it does not express or echo their own cultural experience. Frequently, the true expressions of culture revolve round jokes on the hearing population or on the experience of schooling with the roles reversed. The anger which Benderly (1980) described is expressed in such performances. The rejection of patronizing hearing perceptions or even mistaken views of others with a hearing loss have begun to be addressed:

> The basic problem lying at the heart of deafness can occasionally be overcome by brilliant lip-reading or excellent manual signing. But such a solution is extremely rare. The born deaf child cannot be expected to acquire the subtleties of language with the same easy facility of a hearing child. Manual signing can bridge the gap and it is evident when using manual communication profoundly deaf people have no difficulty in communicating with each other.
>
> (Ashley, 1986, p. vii)

The rejection of these views comes in humour:

> It was Halloween Night at about 8.30. My doorbell flashed for what seemed to be the hundredth time. I groaned and thought, 'what idiot would send their kids out this late?' Grabbing a bowl of candies, I went to the door wondering what costume this kid would be wearing; so far the scariest one was a kid with a Ronald Reagan mask. As I opened the door and glanced down at the kid, I couldn't believe my eyes. I screamed, dropped the bowl, and ran back into the house bolting the door shut behind me. The kid was dressed like a hearing person.
>
> (Bahan, 1989, p. 17)

As it turns out, he is having a series of nightmares about hearingness and even aspects of deafness and sign can be ridiculed:

> 'My girlfriend went to Gallaudet College and returned a different person. I didn't know her, I couldn't even understand her!'

> 'Calm down. Tell me what did she do that you didn't understand?' asked my room-mate soothingly.

> 'I didn't understand her signing. She signed so strange—using signs like ING, WAS THE ...'

(Ibid., p. 18)

In these instances, Deaf people reject the limitations placed on them by hearing people. The jokes are frequently on the fact that the hearing person cannot understand properly. Hearing, like signing, will be ridiculed. Another situation which is frequently called to mind in Deaf stories is the reaction of hearing people when they discover that another adult is deaf. Bahan again:

> 'I am deaf' I said, which is the usual thing I would say to prevent any misunderstanding.

> 'Hi, Dave, I am Susan. Is there anything I can do for you?'

> I suddenly realised she didn't understand me, so I pointed to my ear and shook my head, 'no',

> Susan's face turned pale. I was tempted to say 'boo', but was afraid she would have a heart attack. I could see the newspaper headlines: DEATH MAN SCARED RECEPTIONIST TO DEAF.

(Ibid., p. 29)

It is these aspects of everyday life which form the basis of Deaf culture, shape the perception of the users of BSL and ultimately produce the poetry, drama and stories of the Deaf community. We do not have any written sources in the UK which are as clearly presented as those by Padden and Humphries (1988) and Wilcox (1989) and which have done for UK Deaf culture what these authors have done for American Deaf culture. However, we can learn a great deal from what they have to say and most of it also applies to Deaf culture in Britain.[5]

◀ Activity 10
Stop for a moment and write down a paragraph which describes 'hearing culture'. ◀

◀ Comment
You will find this quite difficult because we do not identify ourselves by the ability to hear. This is a telling point because Deaf people do not consider themselves along the dimension of lack of hearing. You should probably have picked out some characteristic media—radio, television, telephone—and some key points of high culture—opera, concerts. How convincing would these be to a visitor from a different world? We need to begin to think more deeply. ◀

[5] You will find that your readings from Reader One, and the extracts from the videotapes which accompany this course, provide a good source of material on Deaf culture.

Tackling this area continues to be difficult since there is little clear-cut evidence on the culture base of the Deaf community. The comments in this section are rather tentative. Much has been made of the differences between Deaf and hearing culture but it can also be claimed that many of the social customs and traditions are shared between the two communities. In fact, for a great deal of the time the two sets of cultural practices are similar (even when it turns out that the cultural values are different). This is true in major festivals—Christmas, New Year and so on. The same can be said about weddings, births and deaths where church services and receptions follow similar patterns even though (and this is a very significant point) Deaf people will often be unaware of the motives and beliefs of hearing people which are enshrined in the practice. This is a function of a community surrounded and swept along by the customs of the majority. Such occasions are likely to bring to the fore some similar feelings and emotions among Deaf people as among hearing people. However, there are differences which are important and about which social workers in particular have to be sensitive. To tackle these I will consider four rather different aspects: rules of behaviour, customs, traditions and culture itself.

9.1 Rules of behaviour

Hall (1989) has suggested some principles which govern interaction among American Deaf people and which constitute cultural norms for behaviour. A number of her principles have been included in the list for BSL below. Such descriptions may seem, at times, to be no more than a 'tourist's' guide to the Deaf community. However, the means of interaction reflect the underlying experience of being Deaf and are markers of attitude towards Deaf people. Most of the features arise from the exploitation of vision and space rather than sound, but are now firmly identifiable as key aspects of the way Deaf people behave.

1   **Attention-getting and touch:** Deaf people touch each other more than do hearing people (at least in British culture). Entry into a conversation or attention-getting is often done by touch. In British culture we use vocatives (usually the person's name) but this is virtually never done in BSL. Names do not function as vocatives for the obvious reason that signing a name does not bring the person's eye-gaze towards the signer. Touch is used instead and hugs are frequent in greetings between people of the same or opposite sex. Deaf mothers use touch a great deal in early interaction with their deaf and hearing babies—more so than do hearing mothers in Britain.

Touch is permissible in the upper arm (most common), the forearm or shoulder. When sitting next to someone well known and/or where the communication is to be furtive, then touch on the upper leg or thigh is possible. Touch on the front of the body is never allowed except in intimacy. Touch on the back may provoke an angry response—this is an area of cultural conflict as *hearing* norms allow one to touch or push people in the back. Deaf children pushed in the back by hearing children will often treat it as a 'fight signal' and will react violently. Teachers approaching and touching a child from behind will find more than just a startled response.

To attract attention when a person is out of reach, other devices are used such as waving, or even stamping the floor or banging on the table. This latter is less acceptable as it disturbs other people as well. When the attention of a whole audience is required then the lights of the room may be flashed. However, rules governing the use of lights to attract attention are complicated and are discussed further in point 6 below.

2   **Turn-taking** is complex in BSL. During a conversation the signer may look away from the viewer, indicating a wish to continue to hold the floor. The viewer may attempt to contribute to the conversation by waving with a wrist action or by beginning to frame a comment, but it is more likely that facial expression will inform the signer that the viewer wishes to contribute. Turn-taking is generally discussed under a linguistic heading in BSL study and to explain it fully requires more detail than we have space for here.

3   **Breaking into an on-going conversation** is also rule-bound. If two people are signing and a third person appears on the scene and wishes to interrupt to ask the first person about some urgent matter (and it would usually be important or there would be no intrusion), then the format is to touch the first person on the upper arm or shoulder while engaging the *second* person in eye-contact. The person interrupting then directs the signing towards the second person: 'SORRY INTERFERE … ASK' (directed at first person), asks the question of the first person and then turns back to the second person and apologizes again before leaving. The key point is that the person who is interrupting has to address himself or herself to the second signer, not to the person with whom he or she wishes to converse.

4   **Turning away in BSL** is generally an insult and, when attention is called away, the signer has to adopt a convention to ensure that the viewer is not upset. This is often done by signing 'HOLD-ON' or holding the viewer's arm while turning away. Without this it will be seen as a major insult and will often provoke an angry reaction from a Deaf person. It can occur as a conflict between Deaf–hearing norms in the following way: social worker in discussion with a Deaf person is interrupted by a second hearing person—who calls out 'Sorry' or 'Excuse me' and then gives a brief message—to whom the social worker turns (assuming subconsciously that the Deaf person has also been party to the opener of 'Excuse me'). In fact, the reality is that the Deaf person, stopped in mid-flow by the viewer looking away, will become upset. The same is true of telephone interruptions which again, because they are sound based, will not come with any warning to the Deaf person and will, therefore, be treated as insulting if the hearing person simply picks up the telephone in the middle of a conversation. If a Deaf person turns away from another Deaf person in mid-conversation, it will usually signal a serious argument.

5   **Taking another's hands** while he or she is signing is a very aggressive act and similar to covering someone's mouth while talking. Educators have in the past frequently broken this rule in their treatment of deaf children. It prevents articulation and says, 'I don't want to see what you have to say, it is not important'. This is definitely to be avoided as it is a source of much of the cultural anger of Deaf people whose memories of having their arms held down in class will often be vivid.

6   **Use of the light** to gain attention, and 'ringing the doorbell', are further problematical areas governed by Deaf conventions. If a Deaf person wishes to gain the attention of a group of people in a meeting, it is likely that the light switch will be flicked on and on off very briefly once or twice. If this is the final warning or final call to order of the group, the flashing will be more insistent with repetition of very short bursts. Entering a room where a single Deaf person is working or engrossed in a task would usually be preceded by a very brief flick of the main light, on and off. All of these are very short bursts similar to gentle tapping on the door. Lengthening the flashing is equivalent to pounding on a door for a hearing person and is a major irritant. The same rules apply to flashing doorbells when pressing the doorbell for a much longer time keeps everyone in darkness. Sometimes done as a joke among Deaf friends, such a practice is not acceptable from a hearing caller.

7   **Privacy and confidentiality** are more difficult to achieve in the Deaf community because of the general visibility of conversations. Certain topics which are personal will not be discussed in the social area of the Deaf club unless they are already common knowledge. Hearing people, because they liken silent signing to 'whispering' (and assume that others cannot 'hear' conversation) tend to have difficulty in knowing when a topic can be discussed openly. Matters which are seen in the open space of the Deaf club tend to be considered as public knowledge and so can be repeated elsewhere—rumours are easily spread.

Personal matters can be separated from confidential conversations and these, in turn, have to be distinguished from taboo subjects. Just as in the hearing community certain subjects are not to be talked about, so Deaf people tend to have taboos. Some are similar—for example, sexual matters; but others may be different—for example, someone's signing. Personal matters are confidential and social workers may be rejected not because they do not sign, or because the person does not realize help is needed, but because the nature of the situation requires only a very close friend to be involved. Such situations will arise in connection with health, or in personal relations. General confidential topics are probably similar to those among hearing people and concern jobs, finance and so on. In each of the above cases, it is unlikely that conversation will be carried out in an open room.

8   **Leave-taking** in the Deaf community is a lengthy process. Deaf people are usually the last to leave any general gathering as there are always final things to discuss. This may be a function of the lack of alternative remote communication channels but it does mean that Deaf people will continue to converse outside the Deaf club long after the place has been locked up for the night.

This is a brief outline of some of the more commonly encountered aspects of behaviour; it would take a much greater space to give a complete guide to how to behave among Deaf people. As in any new culture, 'be aware that there are different norms for behaviour and be alert for signs of disapproval.'

◄ Activity 11
Write down five rules of behaviour which relate uniquely to hearing culture. ◄

◄ Comment
Other than following the areas described above, you may find this rather difficult. Surely hearing people have some rules of behaviour? You might have mentioned the use of intonation, or the fact that shouting is unacceptable, except in football crowds. Rules about silence in libraries, or on how to knock and enter rooms, may have come to mind. ◄

9.2 Customs

Defining the nature of customs within a community is rather difficult because they may often appear general to the members but yet be rather local in their observation. There is no clear statement of the customs of the Deaf community but we can obtain some pointers from these examples below:

1   **Marriage and weddings:** Although these events are often joint hearing/ Deaf occasions and follow similar patterns, the meaning and performance may be rather different for a Deaf person. It is often said among Deaf people that a wedding has to be a very open event and everyone has to be invited. In effect, it may be more like a 'village' wedding when it was the norm for everyone to join in the celebrations. Customs which are common in hearing weddings, such as after-dinner speeches, are avoided in Deaf-managed weddings. Deaf participants will often seem uninterested in a person signing at the top table (whereas hearing people would stop talking for the speeches). Personal stories about the bride or groom are less likely.

Figure 2.3   'Just married'—A Deaf wedding
(Source: courtesy of the author)

2   **Funerals:** While the general outline of services and practices is dictated by the general community, Deaf people's involvement may be rather different. Church services are part of a hearing culture and although it is normal for Deaf people to attend or request such a service and to have it interpreted, it may be poorly understood in terms of its significance. Deaf people may also be uneasy about any eulogy on the Deaf person who has died as it may be considered tasteless, coming through an interpreter or from a vicar who did not know the person well.

There is no reason to suppose that deaf people feel any less grief following a death (though it is a commonly stated view). The reaction may be confounded by the extent to which the hearing family takes over the organization. However, Deaf people may appear more accepting of the loss and be more prepared to reappear at the Deaf club after only a very short period of mourning. This is difficult to interpret. For a hearing person, the 'club' would be avoided for an appropriate length of time. But that applies to single-purpose associations. The Deaf community encompasses all the interactions of that person in sign, and going to the Deaf club may be precisely the right way to cope with the loss. The fact that it is not then talked about to hearing people is probably part of the distinctions between confidential and personal, as described in Section 9.1 above.

3   **Time and time-keeping:** It is sometimes stated by hearing workers with Deaf people that Deaf people function on a different time-scale and are poor timekeepers. There is no reason to expect that Deaf people's real concept of time is any different from that of hearing people, although one can see that time is expressed very differently in a visual–spatial language. Specifically, time-marking in BSL is realized by setting a time-marker at the beginning of the event or utterance and then all the succeeding action occurs in the 'present tense'. While this may make it difficult for hearing people to determine when an event is occurring, it does not usually cause any problem for Deaf people. The advantage of this system is that it allows the attachment of a very rich system of aspect marking[6] (something which is relatively weaker in English). Failure to 'turn-up' for appointments arises because of lack of clear communication in the first place (about the time, place or importance of the meeting), lack of perceived relevance and lack of a means to cancel or postpone an appointment when a difficulty arises. Sometimes Deaf people will suggest that hearing people have a different concept of time because they tend to rush things. Deaf committee meetings move more slowly because Deaf people want to discuss the matters more fully. A meeting arranged for 8.00 pm could easily begin at 8.15 pm or 8.30 pm without anyone feeling distressed. This may differ from hearing professionals but it is not uncommon in many communities in Britain and is a noticeable feature of rural communities. The implication is that when people meet less frequently or have fewer means of communication outside of face-to-face contact, then there is a great deal of 'business to be transacted' prior to formal meetings.

Appointments made by a Deaf person for someone to visit at his or her home (whether friends, or people coming to deliver or repair

---

[6] See Set Book *Sign Language: The Study of Deaf People and Their Language* by Kyle and Woll, pp. 144–50.

something) invoke customary behaviour. Because of the unreliability of the systems of signalling a person's arrival, Deaf people will abandon their normal daily routine to 'wait near the door'. This will take the form of sitting by the window and frequently glancing outside, or making frequent trips to the door itself. In effect, it causes great disruption to a Deaf person's routine and means that, while someone is expected, very little can be done except this form of 'active waiting'. Not surprisingly, if the expected person arrives very late, the Deaf person can be rather upset, not because it is not possible to understand that other people can be delayed, but rather because a whole period of time has been wasted in needless 'waiting'. Social workers making visits should be very mindful of this issue.

4   **Social customs:** At present these are poorly researched and it is not possible to provide much insight into them. It is customary to have young children at the Deaf club late at night. It is customary to hold surprise parties for anniversaries and birthdays. Deaf people often follow a routine of work, home-to-change and have-a-meal, before going out to the Deaf club. At times people seem fearful of any alteration to this and will be resistant to change or interference by others or even to an invitation to socialize at the 'wrong' time. Fashion is also a feature of Deaf life but it may well be behind that seen amongst hearing people. Lack of information, lack of contact and some conservatism, may make change of clothes, of house decoration and so on, rather slower in the Deaf community. These aspects remain to be described more fully as research on the Community progresses as it is clear that customs of this sort are present in the Deaf community.

9.3 Traditions

As with customs, there has been very little research to inform us of how the traditions of Deaf culture are expressed. At a local level, Christmas parties for deaf children, Christmas meals for elderly people and periodic rallies of Deaf communities are traditional in the sense that they re-occur and have a long history and an important place in the working of the Community. Even where they are derived from an event celebrated by society as a whole, there will have developed a 'Deaf way' of doing it.

Many traditional stories within the Deaf community relate to its development in adversity and revolve around the problems of oralism or of education. Experiences such as those of the deaf children in the schools in the early part of this century, when they were referred to by number rather than by name, are passing into the folklore of the culture. Frequently, Deaf people will use humour to exorcise some of the awful experiences they had in their development and to poke fun at hearing people. Such stories which are 'traditional' among Deaf people at gatherings are part of a dimension which is discussed more fully in Section 9.4 on culture. M.J. Bienvenu's paper on humour, which appeared in *TBC News* in September 1989 and is reproduced overleaf, indicates the Deaf 'tradition' in this respect.

Deaf games are also another feature of cultural life and are an important tradition. Parties are not characterized by loud music as they are in a hearing society but rather by the gradual unfolding of increasingly complex

Reflections of American Deaf Culture in Deaf Humor

Mainstream American culture teaches that "normal" people are born with five senses: hearing, sight, smell, taste and touch. Of course, Deaf people can't hear, and this causes many people to view the Deaf as deficient and deprived. But nothing could be further from the truth—we have always had five senses: sight, smell, taste, touch, and a sense of humor.

Humor is one way that people share their perceptions of the world, express different levels of intimacy, and find comfort in knowing that others share their beliefs. I am going to focus specifically on four categories which reflect the values, norms, and belief systems of our American Deaf Culture.

Visual

As most of you know, Deaf people perceive most things through their eyes. We acquire language visually. It is worth noting that Sign Languages throughout the world adapt to meet the visual needs and comfort of the people who use them. We also acquire world knowledge visually. It should come as no surprise, then, that Deaf humor also has a strong visual base. To many Deaf people, the world is filled with comical sights. But the humor is not always apparent to the majority of hearing Americans.

An experience I had several years ago may illustrate this point: One night while I was co-ordinating an intensive ASL retreat for a group of non-Deaf people, we gathered together to watch the movie *King Kong* on TV. The volume was off, and for the first time, they realized what Deaf audiences have known all along: the actors' expressions are hysterically funny. As New Yorkers were running for their lives with the shadow of a monster ape looming over their heads, our group was laughing uncontrollably. I asked them what they found so funny. They replied, "Their faces!" The same people would have felt frightened if they had heard the actors screaming in terror, with threatening music in the background. Instead, they got a glimpse of the movies from a Deaf perspective.

Deaf people find many visual things humorous which aurally dependent people may not. Often Deaf people are quite creative in their descriptions of people and events. This talent is fostered in residential schools where many children learn the art of storytelling, and most importantly, how to vividly re-create events and characters. When I was in school, no one was safe from our stories. Every identifying characteristic of a person would be imitated, right down to the way s/he walked. This intricate detail is a crucial part of the humor, because it reflects how acutely Deaf people perceive the world, and how adept a tool our language is for expressing our perceptions.

Often people who are not members of the culture will respond negatively to this form of humor. This is a common misunderstanding with outsiders. Deaf people are not insulting the individuals whom we describe; we are delighting in the precision of our language to accurately convey these details. Our culture is reinforced through the shared experience of how we, as a group, see the world and translate it into humor.

Can't Hear

As we all know, deafness is much more than the inability to hear. It is a complete culture, where one's decibel loss is far less important than one's allegiance to the Deaf Community. Yet, a significant amount of Deaf folklore contains jokes and stories which deal with the inability to hear.

There are many stories that have been handed down for generations in Deaf folklore which illustrate the convenience of deafness. The following popular tale shows how Deaf people can solve a problem creatively and humorously: *A Deaf couple arrives at a motel for their honeymoon. After unpacking, the nervous husband goes out to get a drink. When he returns to the motel, he realizes that he has forgotten the room number. It is dark outside and all the rooms look identical. He walks to his car, and leans on the horn. He then waits for the lights to come on in the rooms of the waking angry hearing guests. All the rooms are lit up except his, where his Deaf wife is waiting for him!*

Interestingly, in Ray Holcomb's book, *Hazards of Deafness*, the humor does not follow the culturally Deaf tradition, but rather focuses on stories in which Deaf people lament their "condition." This humor is typical of an "outsider's" view of deafness. Here is an example of one of the scenes in the book: *A deaf person is having a difficult time vacuuming the carpet. He goes over the same spot of dirt repeatedly, to no avail. In a fit of frustration, he turns around and notices that the machine is unplugged.*

This is a perfect example of humor that is *not* Deaf centered. Such a situation would never happen because a Deaf person would naturally feel that the motor was not running and immediately respond appropriately. What is most disturbing is the emphasis on hearing and the dependency on sound which the book portrays. Culturally Deaf people are quite articulate in defining the world in terms other than sound, and have adapted to technology as swiftly as non-Deaf people. The fact that the author does not address Deaf people's keenly developed sense of sight and touch is rather significant.

Linguistic

Another component of Deaf humor can be categorized as linguistic. Production and misproduction of signs is a common way to elicit laughs in ASL. One example, described in Bellugi and Klima's book, *The Signs of Language*, is how we can change the root sign, UNDERSTAND, to LITTLE UNDERSTAND by using the pinkie rather than the index finger.

Much of this linguistic humor is lexically based, and the punch lines to many ASL jokes are related to the production of the words. One of my favorites is the "giant" joke. It is funny both culturally and linguistically: *A huge giant is stalking through a small village of wee people, who are scattering through the streets, trying to escape the ugly creature. The giant notices one particularly beautiful blonde woman scampering down the cobble-stoned street. He stretches out his clumsy arm and sweeps her up, then stares in wonder at the slight, shivering figure in his palm. "You are so beautiful," he exclaims. The young woman looks up in fear. "I would never hurt you," he signs, "I love you! We should get MARRIED." Producing the sign MARRY, he crushes her. The giant then laments, "See, oralism is better."*

There are several components which make this joke successful in American Sign Language. First, it is visually active, because the expressions of the townspeople, the beautiful girl, and the giant can be dramatized to perfection. Secondly, it is linguistically funny because of the sign production MARRY which causes the girl of his affection to splat in his palm. Thirdly, it is humorous in its irony. Culturally Deaf people detest oralism; therefore, the irony in the giant's conclusion that oralism would have saved his beloved girl is funny.

Response to Oppression

It is no secret that Deaf people are an oppressed minority, and one way that minority cultures deal with oppression is through humor. Often this category of humor, sometimes called "zap" stories, features Deaf people getting even.

Often when Deaf people are naturally conversing in public, hearing people will stare at them in disbelief. When they finally gain the courage to initiate conversation with a Deaf person, they will inevitably ask, "Can you read my lips?" Well, of course, Deaf people are keenly aware of the configuration of this one sentence, and will always answer "No!" which is

42

pretty funny, indeed.

Another way Deaf humor fights back at oppression is to show hearing people being outsmarted by a Deaf person. One famous example, which is a true story, provides the required ending: *A group of Deaf people was at a restaurant, chatting away when a group of non-Deaf people at the next table began to rudely mimic their signs. One of the Deaf women decided she'd had enough. She walked to the public telephone, inserted a coin, and making sure she was being observed by the hearing group, signed a complete conversation into the handset, including pauses for the person on the other end to respond. When the Deaf group left the restaurant, they were amused to see the hearing people run over to inspect the phone.*

Deaf people love this one, because we finally have the last laugh. These tales are rich with justice, and always the rude offender is put in her/his place.

In the same way that American Deaf Culture, as well as European Deaf Culture, is oppressed by the majority community, so our language is oppressed. From oralism to Signed English systems and other forms of English/sound coding, Deaf people have suffered under the thumb of hearing educators for many years. From the signs that these "experts" invent, it is obvious they have little knowledge of Deaf Culture or ASL. Often the invented signs already have an established meaning. Many of them look sexual, and are really inappropriate for young children to see, which is ironic, since school systems teach them. It's even worse when they are printed in "sign language" books. Deaf children leaf through these sign-code manuals with delight, snickering at all the "dirty" signs pictured in the textbook.

As one response to these oppressive attempts at linguistic isolation, Deaf people have chosen to incorporate into their discourse some of the artificial codes created from the oral/cued speech/ Signed English systems. Coded signs for IS, AM, ARE, WERE, BE, -ING, -ED, etc. have all been reclaimed by Deaf speakers, and used with sarcasm directed toward those who created them. Of course, the humor is most pronounced when a contorted face accompanies the deviant signs—an editorial on the ineffectiveness of these codes.

In closing, let me say that humor is an essential part of our lives. I'm sure you've all heard the expression, "Laughter is the best medicine." Well, there is much truth to that, particularly when you analyze minority cultures, and realize that they all incorporate fighting back at oppression into their humor. It is a common response to the frustration of our everyday lives, for in humor, the storyteller determines who will "win." Someone told me this joke the other day, and it seemed like a perfect way to end my presentation: *Three people are on a train—one is Russian, one is Cuban, and one is Deaf. The Russian is drinking from a bottle of vodka. She drinks about half the bottle, then throws it out the window. The Deaf person looks at her, surprised. "Why did you throw out a bottle that was only half-empty?" The Russian replies, "Oh, in my country we have plenty of vodka!" Meanwhile, the Cuban is smoking a rich, aromatic cigar. He smokes about half the cigar, then throws it out the window. The Deaf person is again surprised, and asks, "Why did you throw out the cigar?" He replies, "Oh, in Cuba we have plenty of cigars!" The Deaf person nods with interest. A little while later a hearing person walks down the aisle. The Deafie picks him up and tosses him out the window. The Russian and Cuban look up in amazement. The Deaf person shrugs, "Oh, we have plenty of hearing people in the world."*

(Source: Bienvenu, 1989)

Deaf games. These may be quizzes or forfeits or other games designed to catch out the unwary participants, much to the amusement of the group. There is no easy listing or description of these and there is a range of games which are unique to Deaf people, deriving their importance and salience from sign language or the customs and behaviour of Deaf people. Hearing people have a long way to go before they can fully understand them.

There are many other conventions of Deaf culture which will gradually emerge as hearing people stumble across them or as Deaf people become more confident about discussing them. They represent the functioning of a community which is quite different from the hearing/speaking society.

◄ Activity 12
Take a blank sheet of paper and divide it into three sections vertically. In the first column write the name of your cultural group. It could be Scottish, Cornish, Hindu or Jamaican, etc. In the second column write 'hearing' and in the third, 'deaf'. Now list the customs and the traditions of your own culture. Indicate in the second column which of these relate to hearingness and in the final column those in which Deaf people are likely to participate. ◄

◄ Comment
The difficulty that arises in doing an activity like this lies in the fact that your membership of a cultural group (defined by location and by transmission from generation to generation) creates a different idea of tradition.

The generational link among Deaf people is quite different because relatively few have Deaf parents. As a result, participation in society means that Deaf people adapt the traditions they see.

However, you will also have found problems, when considering the hearing column, in identifying anything purely hearing about the traditions. Sound is vital in Christmas carol singing but not in the tradition of family gathering on Christmas Day.

Therefore, traditions do not easily fit the deafness–hearingness dimension. ◀

9.4 Deaf culture

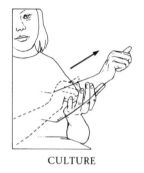

CULTURE

Figure 2.4

Only recently has a sign emerged in BSL for 'culture'. Until then, Deaf people called it the 'DEAF-WAY'. The sign for this latter form involves the hand shape for possession which can be directed at any specific group. Taken together, the three areas mentioned so far (behaviour, customs and traditions) form key parts of the culture of deafness. They do not, however, completely define it. Completing the picture may be some way in the future but we can at least add two aspects: cultural identity (and Deaf pride) and the dimension of deafness–hearingness.

9.4.1 Cultural identity

While the customs and rules of behaviour are outward manifestations of culture, there is an important 'inner' factor which is the extent to which the individual feels part of and comfortable with these practices and experiences. Cultural identity could be measured in some sense by one's adherence to the beliefs and customs of the community. For the Deaf community it is indicated by involvement at the Deaf club and the degree to which a Deaf person seeks out other Deaf people. But it is more than this—it is a sense of closeness to others, a removal of barriers and of the necessity to negotiate the norms of interaction. It is a feeling of shared experience of the world. It is the identity of being Deaf. It is readily recognized not only by the participants but also by those who observe:

> As soon as Clerc beheld this sight (the children at dinner) his face became animated; he was agitated as a traveller of sensibility would be on meeting all of a sudden in distant regions, a colony of his countrymen … Clerc approached them. He made signs and they answered him by signs. This unexpected communication caused a most delicious sensation in them and for us was a scene of expression and sensibility that gave us the most heartfelt satisfaction.
>
> (de Ladebat, 1815)

This is one of the best descriptions of this feeling of identity and it can be retold in nearly every situation in which Deaf people come into contact with each other. It is this experience of relationship which is the central feature of Deaf community and culture.

9.4.2 Deafness–hearingness

One further critical dimension of Deaf community life is its closeness or distance from the hearing norms. Deaf culture has grown in adversity, sometimes with appalling experiences being imposed on very young deaf children, by unknowing parents and by well-intentioned teachers and other professionals. Not surprisingly, Deaf people view their distance from hearing behaviour and custom as a key indicator of their deafness. The nearest we can get to this in hearing culture in the UK is the strength of the term 'sassenach' when applied by some older Scottish people to the English. As a term it draws its vehemence from its onomatopoeic quality and the repeated 's'; it conjures up for Scottish people a period of oppression of both person and of culture which was probably more severe (as it was life-threatening) than that experienced by Deaf people. If we can understand this usage in English, we can begin to get the flavour of the way in which Deaf people define themselves.

On the one hand, 'sassenach' has become more acceptable as a joking term and there is no longer the same antagonism (or at least it is contained within socially acceptable bounds in, say, sporting events). In the same way, Deaf–hearing relations are blurred by the needs of Deaf people to be successful and to master the career structure of a hearing-controlled society. As a result, Deaf people have to accept hearingness in one way because it is only through their understanding of it that they can progress in life. Yet, as Benderly said (in the quotation in Section 3), there is a deep-seated mistrust and misunderstanding of the hearing way. People who are seen to be closer to the hearing way and who are seen to sympathize with it in, for example, education, are often 'written off' by other Deaf people. Yet both Deaf and hearing people are bound together by the larger society. It is something of a paradox and one which our research so far does not disentangle. The Deaf identity has to be seen along a dimension of deafness–hearingness.

The tension this creates is seen in the way that humour is expressed and in the tendency to make fun of hearing people, and, as was discussed at the beginning of Section 9, this is seen in jokes and in plays or mime where it is the hearing person who misunderstands or is made to look foolish. Such devices are important aspects of Community life and are as much expressions of Deaf identity as the more obvious aspects of visual and earthy humour which can be seen. Sometimes, this feeling of reversal becomes more pronounced and more serious as in the paper by Angela Stratly which appeared in *TBC News* in November 1989 and is reproduced overleaf.

Stratiy's point is well made. Hearing-impaired is a relative term. It could just as easily be the other way round. This dimension of deafness–hearingness is a particularly powerful aspect of the early manifestations of Deaf culture. As society becomes more open about the Deaf community and sign language, this emphasis may decline and we will see a rapid expansion of visual art and performance by and for Deaf people.

The Real Meaning of "Hearing Impaired"

For centuries, hearing people in the field of education have labeled deaf children (aka hearing-impaired, deaf mute, deaf and dumb, and hard of hearing) as retarded or delayed in their language development. Charts are frequently developed which compare the language development of hearing and Deaf children and adults. Frequently noted are the low scores of Deaf children and adults in the areas of negatives, conjunctions, question forms, verb conjugation, pronominalization, relative clauses, nominalization, and sentence completion.

As a Deaf teacher of American Sign Language (ASL) as a second language to hearing students, I thought it only appropriate for Deaf people to develop a chart noting the deficiencies of hearing students of ASL (aka severely to profoundly hearing, signing impaired, hard-of-fingerspelling, etc. ...)

Hearing students of ASL frequently have problems with usage. Syntactic errors include: 1) noun-verb pair discrimination (how often have you had to show blow-by-blow the difference between AIRPLANE with a short restrained double movement, and TO-FLY-BY-AIRPLANE with the single continuous movement?), 2) over generalization of sign usage (using the same sign for lose in TO-LOSE-A-GAME and TO-LOSE-A-CAT) 3) poor sign execution (WHY NOT? is often executed to look like two separate thoughts—WHY?? NOT??), 4) weak pluralization (did this student read one book for a long period of time or did this student read a number of books? Was the item shown to one person or was it shown to a crowd?), and 5) inaccurate temporal aspect (did s/he GO somewhere once or did s/he GO-*frequently* to a place? Did s/he CRY-*continuously,* or CRY-HARD?). This poor performance has led to the classification of many severely and profoundly hearing students as **sentence impaired.**

A less severe problem, but one that is common among ASL-as-a-second-language (ASLSL) students is that of inappropriate or inconsistent time markers—a disability which we may refer to as **hard-of-timing.** Errors in this category include the failure to properly produce number incorporation in such semantic items as PAST-WEEK, EVERY-SATURDAY, and ALL-MORNING for example. In addition, hearing students do quite well with expressive fingerspelling, but score miserably on reading it (**hard-of-fingerspelling).**

Locus confusion, a common syndrome among the severely to profoundly hearing, frequently results in misenunciated and misperceived locatives. How often have you wondered when looking at your ASLSL students whether the event being described happened on the side, in front, or in back of the building? This syndrome also causes confused pronominalization.

It is difficult for a **pronoun deprived** hearing person to properly indicate or understand 1) who is speaking to whom, 2) pronouns including or excluding the signer (US-TWO, THREE-OF-THEM ...), and 3) static location on referent nouns. This area of weakness is also reflected in numerous subject/object errors particularly when it is linguistically appropriate to use directional verbs which incorporate subject/object information. We might classify this type of handicap as **misinformed.**

Classifiers are another inherent weakness in the hearing ASLSL student. Due to **dexterity disability** and **sentence impairment,** a hearing person frequently errs in the selection of handshape when attempting to use classifiers. Such an error results in a toothpick being described as having the diameter of a telephone pole or a group of people moving in all directions rather than a mass of people gathered in one location. Another common error is the failure of ASLSL students to shift between real-world and abstract classifiers, resulting in the overuse and over-generalization of such classifiers as 1-CL (*person moving*) and 3-CL (*vehicle moving*). This error often results in an increased number of prayers by ASL teachers to Saint Vitreous Humor for opthomological strength. Since this serious deficit is so common to the profoundly hearing, we label those who suffer from this disability as **misclassified.**

It is the author's opinion that severely to profoundly hearing students produce fingerspelling with approximately 60% accuracy (2nd–3rd grade level), comprehend ASL at a rate of about 40% (4th–5th grade level), and produce ASL at about a 50% level of accuracy (2nd–3rd grade level)—an overall level of performance of 2nd–4th grade level—far below acceptable levels! It is time for Deaf people to unite and provide ASL and visual discrimination remediation clinics for these poor hearing handicapped individuals. Unless we do, teachers will continue to be hired who have only second to third grade Sign Language proficiency and deaf children will continue to suffer under their instruction.

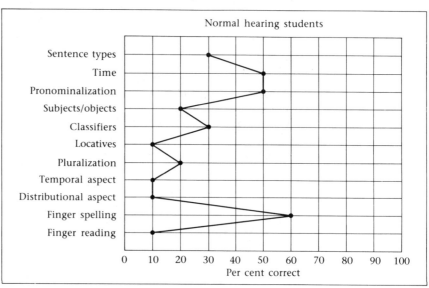

(Source: Stratiy, 1989. Graph developed by Angela Stratiy)

10 The status of the Deaf community

Figure 2.5   Gallaudet struggle created support all across America
(Source: courtesy of Jeff Beatty, photographer)

This is a complicated question as Deaf communities are in different stages of development in different countries and in different parts of the UK. Everywhere there is an increasing awareness and evolving pride in being Deaf, but this is still based on an inadequate knowledge base. The work of the British Sign Language Training Agency in Durham University has done a great deal to set this process in motion.[7] A considerable number of Deaf people have passed through the Agency's training courses, have been prepared to understand their own culture and have gone away much richer and more confident. Nevertheless, there is a great deal of grass-roots development needed to make sure the Deaf population at large has a grasp of its own identity. This is similar to other minority groups and relates to the lack of empowerment which was an earlier theme of this unit.

Such a lack of empowerment should be a thing of the past in view of the major events which took place in Washington in March 1988. Gallaudet University, which is the only Deaf college in the world, appointed a new president. As has been the standard pattern throughout the history of all organizations for Deaf people, the hearing ruling body chose another

---

[7] If you would like to know more about this, see Article 6.7 'British Sign Language Tutor Training Course' by A.C. Denmark in Reader Two.

hearing person for the post. Immediately, this produced a great student protest movement, which was likened to the civil rights movement in the 1960s. As well as being perfectly organized internally and being able to bring the University to a standstill, the protesters were able to enlist the sympathies of the nation, and in particular to mobilize, on their behalf, the politicians in Washington. As a result, they were able to force the reversal of the decision to appoint a hearing person and had a Deaf president installed. For the Deaf community in general this was a historic and momentous event—as the extract from *The New York Times* opposite illustrates—which should have had a major impact across the world.

The 'Deaf President Now' protest caught the attention of all the US press. Unfortunately, there has been no spreading revolution and no re-statement of the rights of Deaf people in any other country. As we move into the 1990s, virtually all of the large national Deaf organizations have hearing chief executives. Virtually all the centres for the Deaf have hearing principals. Why? Because the hearing person appointed always had the best qualifications. Such a statement fails to understand the need for the Deaf community to be meaningfully represented and for Deaf culture to be modelled and presented in the institutions which are seen by administrators and by legislators. **The qualification of deafness is a fundamental necessity in such circumstances and a clarity of identity and belief in the culture is vital**.

Everything written in the previous sections of this unit is negated when such decisions are taken by the powerful hearing majority. Cultures and identity are bound up in the experience of deafness and it is this aspect which has to be seen and understood by those decision-makers. If the hearing majority fail to take the opportunity to understand, they will continue to misunderstand Deaf people, to deny their language and culture, and will accentuate their own hearing ethnocentricity.

Protest That Turned Campus for the Deaf Around

WASHINGTON, March 14— The United States has seen its full share of campus protests, particularly over the last 25 years.

But seldom, if ever, has the nation seen a campus upheaval quite like the one that culminated Sunday night at Gallaudet University, the country's only liberal arts college for the deaf.

Other university and college protests have usually had relatively limited goals and mixed endings: a dean removed, a restriction modified, mass arrests because of violence.

At Gallaudet, by contrast, the goal was nothing less than the restructuring of the way an institution operated. The deaf— not just students but also faculty members and alumni and, in the end, deaf people from around the nation—demanded that the hearing surrender to them control of what is perhaps the foremost university in the world for the deaf. Remarkably, they achieved almost all their demands, and in the very short time of a single week. How? Why?

Complex Explanation
Their campaign was well planned. It was run with sophistication. The opposition seem alternately insensitive and impolitic. But the explanation for the success of the protest is considerably more complex than that.

At first glance, it seemed to center on Gallaudet and academia. In fact, Gallaudet was only a convenient symbol for the protesters, a bitterly ironic place that boasted of a special ability to train deaf people for the working world but itself refused to hire a deaf person for its top job.

Gallaudet, which had been set up to help solve a problem, had become part of the problem. In acting, the protesters served notice from its grounds that deaf people everywhere, not just at Gallaudet, were weary of being treated like children, that they were tired of paternalism and condescension, even "oppression" by the hearing.

They said they wanted control of their own destiny and that Gallaudet University, run by the hearing for all its 124 years, was where they intended to take the first step toward seizing that control.

The Appeal Snowballs
It turned out to be an exceptionally appealing call to arms, appealing to an extent that fooled even the protest organizers. Within hours the students who had started the protest had been joined by a majority of their faculty. Then the Gallaudet alumni climbed on board, followed by consumer groups, labor unions and politicians.

Gallaudet, in the larger sense, was a protest whose time had come. It is now clear that the protesters, particularly the students who initiated the demonstration that shut down the campus for the week, were the shock troops in the first major battle of a national campaign to obtain more civil rights and opportunities for the nation's millions of deaf people.

Specifically, the protesters took strong exception to an effort by the university to install still another president who suffered no hearing impairment and did not know sign language. She was Elisabeth Ann Zinser, a highly regarded North Carolina educator.

The protesters were unmoved by her considerable reputation. How, they asked, could someone like that, however qualified as an academician and administrator, truly understand Gallaudet? How, they asked, could such a choice be made?

Inadequate Responses
The answers that came back not only did not satisfy the protesters but also infuriated them. In retrospect, they were answers that also helped the protesters achieve their victory. At best many seemed tinged with an unawareness of what was happening in the world of the deaf and, at worst, with outright insensitivity.

The chairman of the Gallaudet board, Jane Bassett Spilman, argued steadfastly that a person who was not deaf could run a university for the deaf as well as anybody. She steadfastly maintained that the board, made up like most university boards of the wealthy, influential and issue-oriented, need not be reconstituted even though only four of its 21 members had hearing difficulties.

Then, in what was perhaps one of two break points in the dispute—the other came when more than half the faculty came out against Dr. Zinser's appointment—Mrs. Spilman was quoted as saying that "deaf people are not ready to function in a hearing world." Initially she denied the quotation. Later she said she had mistakenly used a "double negative" and thus may have mistakenly left the impression that she held such an opinion.

Whatever the case, Mrs. Spilman was never able thereafter to get off the defensive. Further, the more she defended herself, Dr. Zinser and her board, the worse the situation seemed to grow.

Then came the faculty vote, a well timed move that Dr. Zinser subsequently acknowledged made it almost imperative that she pull out. She did, announcing her decision at 1 o'clock one morning, for reasons that were never entirely clear but nevertheless seemed in perfect keeping with the confusion surrounding the Gallaudet situation.

What the Protesters Won
The results of Sunday's board meeting were perhaps the most surprising development of all. For in the end, the protesters won almost all of their demands.

They got a new president. I. King Jordan, dean of the Gallaudet School of Arts and Sciences, and a new board chairman, Philip Bravin, a New York business executive, both deaf. They also won a promise that the board would be restructured to include more deaf people. And they even won a promise of amnesty for all students and faculty who had participated in the protest.

by B. Drummond Ayres Jr.

Paul A Sounders, The New York Times

Dr I King Jordan, the first deaf president of Gallaudet University, being greeted by students …

(Source: from the front page of *The New York Times*, 15 March 1988)

11 The gift of deafness

The value of deafness is quite different from the existence of hearing loss and can be seen in the development of its own culture and in the evolution of a rich and complex language. The fact that this culture is beginning to be expressed publicly means that Deaf people are now more willing to share this gift and view of the world with a wider audience. Acceptance of this message is the beginning of a meaningful integration which is not submersion. The correct terminology would be 'accommodation' where the wider community accepts and learns from Deaf culture. Deaf people have a unique visual involvement in the world. The talent that goes with this view should never have been suppressed—it tells us about language in general and it characterizes all social interaction with great insight. The world at large is not a hearing world but a world which is a mosaic of communities, each contributing. The Deaf community is one such community.

> She looked a bit irritated, and said 'why don't you speak?' while pointing to her lips.
>
> I thought 'she must be one of those wackos', and proceeded to squirm my slimy tongue around its oral cavity and uttered, 'Un hs .. hagmerbersugar uth kees'.
>
> She suddenly looked bewildered, and turned to look at the menu. She took my order and left.
>
> Fifteen minutes later she came back with my cheeseburger and a note. I read the note and it said 'I have a deaf brother who went to a wonderful school up north. Now he speeks wel, you know you shoold lern to speek. Its nevar to lat. Aftar al you lif in a hearing wurld.'
>
> I read her note and wondered where she learned to write. But as I read on I thought 'what right does she have to claim, without asking me, that I did not receive speech training'. After all, I went to a school that incorporates this method in its School Philosophy ...
>
> I pondered on that issue. What right do hearing people have to impose on us the dominance of their world? What is even worse, there are deaf people who strongly uphold hearing world values on us deaf people. They go around saying you have to learn to speak because it is a hearing world. It's strange because while they use that phrase, they are denying their own existence as a deaf person. If the world is not theirs, then who are they?
>
> I am proposing for us all to go out and say, 'Hell, it's our world, too!' Of course I cannot deny the fact that there are more, many more, hearing people than there are deaf. But I can and will deny them the right to claim the world.
>
> (Bahan, 1989, pp. 45–7)

Suggestions for further reading

KYLE, J.G. and WOLL, B. (1985) *Sign Language: The study of Deaf People and Their Language*, Cambridge, Cambridge University Press.

This is already one of your Set Books. It describes the language and also the Community. Do read Appendix 1 which is a Deaf account of growing up and of involvement in the Community.

SACKS, O. (1989) *Seeing Voices*, London, Picador.

This is an account of a journey of exploration into the world of Deaf people. It is of considerable interest because it does explore and it does comment on the situation of Deaf people in a way which brings the experience to life.

VAN CLEEVE, J.V. and CROUCH, B.A. (1989) *A Place of Their Own: Creating the Deaf Community in America*, Washington, DC, Gallaudet University Press.

Although this is an American account of history, it is illuminating in its description of the struggle for recognition amongst Deaf people.

WILCOX, S. (1989) *American Deaf Culture*, Silver Spring, MD, Linstok.

More than any book so far this one captures the Deaf experience in a very direct and challenging way. This collection is essential reading for the student of culture and community.

References

ABBERLEY, P. (1987) 'Concept of oppression: development of social theory of disability', *Disability, Handicap and Society*, vol. 1, pp. 25–9.

ASHLEY, J. (1986) 'Foreword', in Sainsbury, S. *Deaf Worlds: A Study of Integration, Segregation and Disability*, London, Hutchinson.

AYRES, JR, B.D. (1988) 'Protest that turned campus for the deaf around', *The New York Times*, 15 March.

BAHAN, B. (1989) 'Various extracts from Deaf Community News', in Wilcox, S. (ed.) *American Deaf Culture*, Silver Spring, MD, Linstok.

BAKER, C. and COKELY, D. (1980) *ASL: A Teacher's Resource Text on Grammar and Culture*, Silver Spring, MD, T.J. Publishers.

BAKER, C. and PADDEN, C. (1978) 'Focussing on the non-manual components of ASL', in Siple, P. (ed.) *Understanding Language Through Sign Language Research*, New York, Academic Press.

BARTON, L. (1989a) *Disability and Dependency*, Lewes, Falmer Press.

BARTON, L. (1989b) *Integration: Myth or Reality*, Lewes, Falmer Press.

BATSON, T.W. and BERGMAN, E. (1976) *The Deaf Experience*, South Waterford, ME, Merriam-Eddy.

BELL, A.G. (1884) *Memoir upon the Formation of a Deaf Variety of the Human Race*, Washington, DC, National Academy of Sciences.

BENDERLY, B.L. (1980) *Dancing Without Music*, New York, Anchor Press.

BIENVENU, M.J. (1989) 'Reflections of American deaf culture in deaf humor', *The Bicultural Center News*, September, no. 17.

BOOTH, T. (1988) 'Challenging conceptions of integration', in Gregory, S. and Hartley, G.M. (eds) (1990) *Constructing Deafness*, London, Pinter Publishers. (D251 Reader Two, Article 5.10)

BRECHIN, A. and WALMSLEY, J. (1989) *Making Connections: Reflecting on the Lives and Experiences of People with Learning Difficulties*, London, Hodder and Stoughton.

BULLARD, D. (1986) *Islay*, Silver Springs, MD, T.J. Publishers.

CHRISTIANSEN, J. (1982) 'The socioeconomic status of the deaf community, a review', in Christiansen, J. and Egelston-Dodd, J. (eds) *Working Papers no. 4, Socioeconomic Status of the Deaf Population,* Washington, DC, Gallaudet College.

CONRAD, R. (1979) *The Deaf School Child*, London, Harper and Row.

DE LADEBAT, L. (1815) *Collection of Most Remarkable Definitions of Massieu and Clerc*, London, Cox and Bayliss.

FIRTH, G.C. (1989) *Chosen Vessels*, Sydney Rd, Exeter, G.C. Firth.

FOSTER, S. (1986) *Employment Experiences of Deaf RIT Graduates, an Interview Study*, Rochester, NY, NTID Occasional Papers.

GRANT, B. (1987) *The Quiet Ear: Deafness in Literature*, London, Andre Deutsch.

GREGORY, S. and BARLOW, S. (1989) 'Interactions between Deaf babies and their Deaf and hearing mothers', in Woll, B. (ed.) *Language Development and Sign Language*, Monograph no.1, International Sign Linguistics Association, Bristol, Centre for Deaf Studies.

GREGORY, S. and BISHOP, J. (1989) 'The mainstreaming of primary age deaf children', in Gregory, S. and Hartley, G.M. (eds) (1990) *Constructing Deafness*, London, Pinter Publishers. (D251 Reader Two, Article 5.11)

GREGORY, S. and HARTLEY, G.M. (eds) (1990) *Constructing Deafness*, London, Pinter Publishers. (D251 Reader Two)

GROCE, N.E. (1985) 'Everyone here spoke sign language', in Gregory, S. and Hartley, G.M. (eds) (1990) *Constructing Deafness*, London, Pinter Publishers. (D251 Reader Two, Article 1.2)

HALL, S. (1989) 'TRAIN-GONE-SORRY: the etiquette of social conversations in American Sign Language', in Wilcox, S. *American Deaf Culture*, Silver Spring, MD, Linstok.

HARRIS, R. and STIRLING, L. (1986) 'Developing and defining an identity', in Christiansen, J.B. and Meisegeir, R.W. (eds) *Second Research Conference on Social Aspects of Deafness*, Washington, DC, Gallaudet College Press.

HASE, U. (1987) 'Hearing tactics in the adjustment of the deafened', in Kyle, J.G. (ed.) *Adjustment to Acquired Hearing Loss*, Bristol, University of Bristol, Centre for Deaf Studies.

HIGGINS, P. (1980a) *Outsiders in a Hearing World: a Sociology of Deafness*, New York and London, Sage.

HIGGINS, P. (1980b) 'Outsiders in a hearing world', in Gregory, S. and Hartley, G.M. (eds) (1990) *Constructing Deafness*, London, Pinter Publishers. (D251 Reader Two, Article 2.1)

HILLERY, G. (1974) *Communal Organisations*, Chicago, IL, Chicago University Press.

HODGSON, K.W. (1954) *The Deaf and Their Problems*, London, Watts.

JACKSON, P. (1986) *The Deaf Community: Final Report to British Deaf Association*, Carlisle, British Deaf Association.

JACOBS, L.M. (1980) *A Deaf Adult Speaks Out*, Washington, DC, Gallaudet College Press.

JONES, L., KYLE, J.G. and WOOD, P. (1987) *Words Apart: Losing Your Hearing as an Adult*, London, Tavistock.

JONES, L. and PULLEN, G. (1987) *Inside We Are All Equal: Social Policy Survey of Deaf People*, Bristol, Bristol University School of Education.

KYLE, J.G. (1987) *Adjustment to Acquired Hearing Loss*, Bristol, University of Bristol, Centre for Deaf Studies.

KYLE, J.G. and ALLSOP, L. (1982) *Deaf People and the Community, Final Report to Nuffield*, Bristol, Bristol University School of Education.

KYLE, J.G. and PULLEN, G. (1985) *Young Deaf People in Employment, Final Report to MRC*, Bristol, Bristol University School of Education.

KYLE, J.G. and WOLL, B. (1985) *Sign Language: The Study of Deaf People and Their Language*, Cambridge, Cambridge University Press. (D251 Set Book)

KYLE, J.G., WOLL, B. and LLEWELLYN-JONES, P. (1981) 'Learning and using BSL, current skills and training', *Sign Language Studies*, vol. 31, pp. 155–78.

KYLE, J.G. and WOOD, P.L. (1983) *Social and Vocational Aspects of Acquired Hearing Loss*, Bristol, Bristol University School of Education.

LADD, P. (1981) 'Making plans for Nigel: the erosion of identity by mainstreaming', in Taylor, G. and Bishop, J. (eds) (1990) *Being Deaf: The Experience of Deafness*, London, Pinter Publishers. (D251 Reader One, Article 10)

LADD, P. (1988) 'The modern Deaf community', in Gregory, S. and Hartley, G.M. (eds) (1990) *Constructing Deafness*, London, Pinter Publishers. (D251 Reader Two, Article 2.3)

LANE, H. (1984a) *When the Mind Hears,* New York, Random House.

LANE, H. (1984b) *The Deaf Experience*, Cambridge, MA, Harvard University Press.

LAWSON, L. (1981) 'The role of sign in the structure of the Deaf community', in Woll, B., Kyle, J.G. and Deuchar, M. (eds) *Perspectives on BSL and Deafness*, London, Croom Helm.

LUCKMAN, B. (1970) 'The small life-worlds of modern man', *Social Research,* vol. 37, pp. 580–96.

MCLOUGHLIN, M.G. (1987) *A History of the Education of the Deaf in England*, Liverpool, G.M. McLoughlin.

PADDEN, C. (1980a) 'The Deaf community and the culture of Deaf people', in Baker, C. and Battison, R. (eds) *Sign Language and the Deaf Community*, Silver Spring, MD, National Association of the Deaf.

PADDEN, C. (1980b) 'The Deaf community and the culture of Deaf people', in Gregory, S. and Hartley, G.M. (eds) (1990) *Constructing Deafness*, London, Pinter Publishers. (D251 Reader Two, Article 2.4)

PADDEN, C. and HUMPHRIES, T. (1988) *Voices for Deaf Culture*, Berkeley, CA, University of California Press.

RNID (1988) *Communication Works: Inquiry into the Employment of Deaf People*, London, RNID.

ROBINSON, J. (1989) 'Deaf pride: quest for a place in a hearing world', *ECRS Journal,* 3 July, pp. 6–7.

SAINSBURY, S. (1986) *Deaf Worlds: A Study of Integration, Segregation and Disability*, London, Hutchinson.

SCHEIN, J.D. (1987) 'The demography of deafness', in Higgins, P. and Nash, J.E. (eds) *Understanding Deafness Socially*, Springfield, IL, Charles Thomas.

SCHEIN, J.D. and DELK, M.T. (1974) *The Deaf Population of the United States*, Silver Spring, MD, National Association of the Deaf.

SCOTT, W.C. (1870) *The Deaf and Dumb*, London, Bell and Daldy.

SCOUTEN, E.L. (1984) *Turning Points in the Education of Deaf People*, Danville, IL, Interstate.

STINSON, M. (1970) *Personality, Family Background and Job Success of Deaf Adults*, Ann Arbor, MI, Unpublished Doctoral Dissertation, University of Michigan.

STRATIY, A. (1989) 'The real meaning of "hearing-impaired"', *The Bicultural Center News*, November, no. 19.

TAYLOR, G. and BISHOP, J. (eds) (1990) *Being Deaf: The Experience of Deafness*, London, Pinter Publishers. (D251 Reader One)

THOMAS, D. (1982) *The Experience of Handicap*, London, Methuen.

VAN CLEEVE, J.V. and CROUCH, B.A. (1989) *A Place of Their Own: Creating the Deaf Community in America*, Washington, DC, Gallaudet University Press.

WILCOX, S. (1989) *American Deaf Culture*, Silver Spring, MD, Linstok.

WOOLLEY, M. (1987) 'Acquired hearing loss—acquired oppression', in Taylor, G. and Bishop, J. (eds) (1990) *Being Deaf: The Experience of Deafness*, London, Pinter Publishers. (D251 Reader One, Article 31)

YOUNG, J. (1989) 'Deaf pride: our honorary director responds', *ECRS Journal*, 3 July, p. 7.

Acknowledgements

Grateful acknowledgement is made to the following sources for permission to reproduce material in this unit:

Text
Bienvenu, M.J. (1989) 'Reflections of American deaf culture in deaf humor', *The Bicultural Center News*, no. 17, September 1989, The Bicultural Center; Stratiy, A. (1989) 'The real meaning of "hearing impaired"', *The Bicultural Center News*, no. 19, November 1989, The Bicultural Center; Ayres, Jr, B.D. (1988) 'Protest that turned campus for the deaf around', *The New York Times*, 15 March 1988, copyright © 1988 by The New York Times Company. Reprinted by permission.

Figures
Figure 2.2 The Science Museum, London, negative no. 293/59; *Figure 2.5* copyright © by Jeff Beatty, Whiteoak, Maryland, USA.

Grateful acknowledgement is made to Trevor Landell for permission to use his painting on the covers and title pages throughout the units of this course.

Unit 3 British Sign Language, Communication and Deafness

prepared for the course team by Susan Gregory and Dorothy Miles

Contents

Associated study materials

Videos: As all the videos show aspects of British Sign Language and communication with Deaf people, all provide useful background material for this unit. However, Video Two, *Sign Language,* was produced in conjunction with this unit, and this video is studied in detail in this part of the course.

Reader One, Article 5, 'Total Commitment to Total Communication', Riki Kittel.

Reader One, Article 7, 'Deafness: the Treatment', Lorraine Fletcher.

Reader Two, Article 1.2, 'Everyone Here Spoke Sign Languare', Nora Groce.

Reader Two, Section 6, *The Linguistic Perspective* (reference is also made to Section 2, parts of which were studied in connection with Unit 2).

Set Book: D. Miles, *British Sign Language: A Beginner's Guide*, pp. 15–26, Chapter 3 (pp. 44–106).

Set Book: J. Kyle and B. Woll, *Sign Language: The Study of Deaf People and Their Language*, pp. 48–57.

D251 Issues in Deafness

Unit 1   *Perspectives on Deafness: An Introduction*

Block 1   **Being Deaf**
Unit 2   *The Deaf Community*
Unit 3   *British Sign Language, Communication and Deafness*
Unit 4   *The Other Deaf Community?*

Block 2   **Deaf People in Hearing Worlds**
Unit 5   *Education and Deaf People: Learning to Communicate or Communicating to Learn?*
Unit 6   *The Manufacture of Disadvantage*
Unit 7   *Whose Welfare?*

Block 3   **Constructing Deafness**
Unit 8   *The Social Construction of Deafness*
Unit 9   *Deaf People as a Minority Group: The Political Process*
Unit 10   *Deaf Futures*

Readers
Reader One: Taylor, G. and Bishop, J. (eds) (1990) *Being Deaf: The Experience of Deafness*, London, Pinter Publishers.
Reader Two: Gregory, S. and Hartley, G.M. (eds) (1990) *Constructing Deafness*, London, Pinter Publishers.

Set Books
Kyle, J. and Woll, B. (1985) *Sign Language: The Study of Deaf People and Their Language*, Cambridge, Cambridge University Press.
Miles, D. (1988) *British Sign Language: A Beginner's Guide*, London, BBC Books (BBC Enterprises). With a chapter by Paddy Ladd.

Videotapes
Video One   *Sandra's Story: The History of a Deaf Family*
Video Two   *Sign Language*
Video Three *Deaf People and Mental Health*
Video Four   *Signs of Change: Politics and the Deaf Community*

Aims

The aims of this unit are unusual in that they start by indicating an aim which is not part of the unit. It is not intended to teach British Sign Language (BSL), and those of you who have no knowledge of the language are not expected to learn it, although in order to appreciate some of the discussion you will need to become familiar with some of its features. A section of the unit is set aside for this. Even if it were desirable that you should learn British Sign Language by studying this unit, it would not be possible, as language acquisition—particularly for a visual–gestural language with no written form, such as BSL—requires contact with users of the language.[1]

The aims of this unit are:
1   To explore the relationship between language and culture.
2   To describe some of the general features of languages.
3   To describe features of British Sign Language.
4   To examine the range and variety of language used by deaf people.
5   To show how British Sign Language is acquired by children and adults.
6   To examine the process of interpreting between British Sign Language and English.
7   To look at the relationship between power and language and minority groups.

Study guide

Because this unit is about British Sign Language, it draws heavily on video material (the same material being used in different ways throughout), Reader articles and Set Books. It also makes extensive use of activities which are seen as an integral part of the work for this section of the course. This means that studying this unit requires particularly careful planning. We suggest that you go through the unit carefully, noting the activities (particularly those involving another person) and the use of video material and readings, so that you can plan your work to fit your circumstances. It may be helpful, for example, to view all the video material first, or to leave all the Reader articles to the end.

A suggested plan for study would be:

Week one
Review unit.

Study Sections 1–4, to gain or increase your understanding of BSL.

Week two
Study Sections 5–8, looking at misconceptions about sign language and sign language as it is used.

Week three
Study Sections 9–12, looking at the acquisition of sign language, and language and power. You should have time to review the unit at the end of this week, perhaps by reviewing the video.

---

[1] If you do not know British Sign Language but would like to learn it, the *Study Skills and Resource Booklet* will give you ideas on how you might pursue this.

1 Language and culture

You can cut off the fingers of deaf people and they will sign with their arms, and you can cut off their arms and they will sign with their shoulders.
(Reported by Hans Furth, 1973, in *Deafness and Learning: A Psychosocial Approach*)

In the last unit the Deaf community and Deaf culture were described. One of the main defining elements of Deaf culture is its language, which for the British Deaf community is British Sign Language or BSL. Most definitions of the Deaf community stress the importance of sharing a common language. This is emphasized in the articles in Reader Two, Section 2 'Defining the Deaf Community'. Deaf culture was described in Unit 2 partly in terms of its stories, humour, games and traditions, all of which are interwoven with the language of Deaf people—sign language.

In all societies, language and culture are inextricably bound up together, with each being a reflection of the other. The relationship between them can be understood in two complementary ways: on the one hand the language reflects and describes the culture in which it is used, while on the other, and at the same time, it constructs that society. One way to appreciate this is to draw an analogy with advertising. Television commercials are often criticized for making people want the products advertised—for creating a need. The advertiser's response is often to say that they only reflect society, that they can only work because they show to people images with which they can easily identify. We would want to say that both processes are occurring together.

The power of language to reflect the society in which it is used and to construct its reality is an important concept. Some languages talk of concepts that would not be meaningful in others. Roy Harris gives the following examples:

> Most Europeans would be puzzled to know how to reply if asked the question 'What is the word in your language for what people say on Thursdays?' or 'What do you call the words spoken at night?' or 'What do you call talk that took place a year ago?' But these questions would make perfectly good sense to a Mayan Indian of Tenejapa, whose language, Tzeltal, provides commonly used designations for all of these. It is not that the European lacks the linguistic resources to make up a translation such as 'Thursday talk' or 'nightwords'; but rather that he (*sic*) would be at a loss to understand the point of drawing such distinctions. It is not part of his (*sic*) concept of a language that a language should provide you with Thursday talk or night words, and if it does not do that then it need provide no corresponding metalinguistic expressions either.
>
> (Harris, 1980)

There is a sense in which the sharing of experience involves being able to talk about the experience, and to give name to it. Virginia Woolf talks of the difficulty of understanding and explaining pain:

English which can express the thoughts of Hamlet and the tragedy of Lear has no words for the shiver or the headache ... The merest schoolgirl when she falls in love has Shakespeare or Keats to speak her mind for her, but let the sufferer try to describe a pain in the head to a doctor and language at once runs dry.

(Woolf, 1967)

In both these examples, language as the medium of expression can be seen as reflecting the society in which it is used and, at the same time, as constructing that reality by specifying what is or is not significant. Yet this is not the whole story, for it presents a static view of language and culture which does not account for change. It also does not recognize variations of language use within a society or of the power relations these can represent. Individuals experience society differently depending upon their status within that society, for language also serves to describe and maintain power relations within and between cultural groups. Feminists, for example, have long argued that the male-centred language not only defines or describes a male-dominated society, but also serves to maintain such power relationships and to sustain the male-dominated culture.

There is a further way in which language is linked to culture in that it can bind together a group of people and set them aside from the rest of the population. Professional and occupational groups are often accused of using jargon—particular forms of language which exclude others, and which serve to maintain the group identity and set it apart. The Open University itself has its own language of TMAs and D251 which can be incomprehensible to the outsider. Likewise, the special language of Deaf people can unite Deaf people, while at the same time setting them aside from hearing people. As Barbara Kannapell says in writing about American Sign Language (ASL), though she could equally well be writing about BSL:

ASL has a unifying function, since deaf people are unified by their common language. But the use of ASL simultaneously separates deaf people from the hearing world. So the two functions are different perspectives on the same reality—one from inside the group which is unified, and the other from outside. The group is separated from the hearing world. This separatist function is a protection for deaf people. For example, we can talk about anything we want, right in the middle of a crowd of hearing people. They are supposed not to understand us. It is important to understand that ASL is the only thing we have that belongs to deaf people completely. It is the only thing that has grown out of the deaf group. Maybe we are afraid to share our language with hearing people. Maybe our group identity will disappear once hearing people know ASL.

(Kannapell, 1980)

2 The study of language

In order to pursue discussions of the relationship between language and culture further, however, we must ask, 'What is language?', and in our consideration of BSL we shall also have to ask, 'What are its features such that we can consider it to be a language?'. In order to do this it is important to be clear about what language is.

ITQ

How would you define language?

What do you consider to be its essential features?

In thinking about this you may find it useful to think about animal communication, computer languages, and communication systems such as tick-tack (racecourse semaphore signalling) or those used by television producers etc.

We shall be considering this issue in various ways throughout the unit and you may wish to return to this ITQ again at the end.

As Roy Harris points out, there is something odd about the question 'What is language?' because it is posed in language and can only be answered in language, and something of what language is must be understood by anyone who could ask such a question. He notes that it is similar to: '... a traveller who inquires of other passengers standing on platform one whether any of them can tell him the way to the station' (Harris, 1980).

There are, of course, many ways of answering such a question, but for our discussion here we will highlight just two features which are generally recognized as important characteristics of language. These derive from the work of de Saussure, the Swiss linguist sometimes known as the father of modern linguistics.

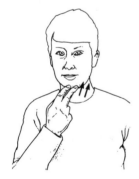

Figure 3.1 BSL sign for UNCLE

The first of these features is that the elements (words or signs) of a language are arbitrary—there is no direct relationship between an element and that which it signifies. For de Saussure, language is a system of 'linguistic elements'.[2] An essential feature of the linguistic element is that it is arbitrary—that is, there is no reason why a particular word or sign should be used rather than any other. The BSL sign for 'uncle' is shown in Figure 3.1[3]—but there is no reason why other hand configurations or movements should not be used: this particular sign is arbitrary. Likewise, the word 'uncle' could be replaced by 'jat' or 'nicheban' or any other sound—it does not have to be 'uncle'. Further evidence for this lies in the fact that different languages give the same item a different word or sign, as Figure 3.2 illustrates.

[2]The common word for linguistic element, and the word used throughout de Saussure is 'sign'. However, in a unit on sign language, the use of this word potentially generates such confusion that we have chosen to speak of 'linguistic elements'.

[3]You will notice that all the individual participants in the BSL illustrations are white. While the course team recognizes that Black and Asian people use sign language, we felt it wrong to suggest by implication that that language would be BSL.

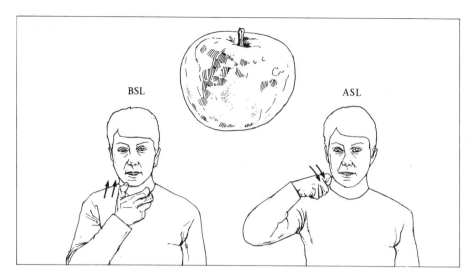

Figure 3.2   APPLE, POMME (French), ALMA (Hungarian)

Furthermore, different languages do not divide up the world in the same way. In English there is a distinction between river and stream in terms of the amount of water in each. In French the distinction is between 'fleuve' which flows into the sea, and 'rivière' which does not. Thus, there is not a one-to-one relationship between languages, each linguistic element of one matching a linguistic element of another. Languages do not name already existing categories, but create their own.

The second feature is that in an utterance (either signed or spoken) there is a systematic relationship between the linguistic elements which are rule governed. Meaning is conveyed not only by the linguistic elements, but by the relationship between them in the utterance—the syntax or grammar. For example, 'John hit Mary' does not mean the same as 'Mary hit John'. Likewise, 'Sadly, John returned here' is different from 'John returned here sadly'. The difference lies not in the words themselves, which are the same, but in the order or the structure of the sentence. Before de Saussure, the study of language was the study of the history and derivation of particular words, but he emphasized the need to study a language as a system as it exists at a particular time.

3 Visual–gestural communication

Before going on to consider British Sign Language in some detail, we would like you to think about visual–gestural communication. Most of us have gestures within our repertoire—a wave for a 'good-bye', a beckoning for 'come here', a nod of the head for 'yes' and a shake for 'no'. These gestures are cultural and not universal. For example, in Albania a shake of the head means 'yes' and a nod 'no', the reverse of most Western European countries, which can make declining or accepting the offer of food or drink an effort in conscious control!

Figure 3.3(a)

There now follows a number of exercises to encourage you to start thinking about visual–gestural communication. We strongly recommend that you do these as a way of starting to think (or clarifying your thinking) about visual–gestural communications. However, you should not be misled into thinking that you are using a language, or that British Sign Language, because it uses the visual–gestural mode, is simple. The point of the exercise is to consider the effects of the modality.

◄ Activity 1

Note: You may be tempted to skip these activities. However, the attempt to do them will make the following section on British Sign Language easier to understand and appreciate.

You will need to work with someone else to do this. If you can sign yourself, your partner should not be able to.

(a) First, you must convey to your partner the following items—you may not use pen or paper or other material, or show the page, or point to objects in the room. Those of you who know the game 'Give us a Clue' should resist the temptation to use the conventions of that game (e.g. to use fingers to indicate the number of syllables, or to break the word down into constituent parts, or indicate 'sounds like').

table	woman	scissors	sun	photograph
aeroplane	man	paper	telephone	apple
tea	jealousy	mother	toy	sister

(b) You and your partner should now use the two identical pictures, which are Figure 3.3(a) in the text here and Figure 3.3(b) supplied at the end of the unit, and choose, in turn, an object or person on the picture and convey your choice to your partner without pointing. Try this several times.

(c) Convey the following story to your partner by visual–gestural means:

> Yesterday I went for a walk in the wood. At the beginning the trees were small and far apart. As I went further in they were taller and closer together. It was dark. I was frightened. I ran out. I discovered I had lost my watch. Tomorrow I will go and look for it.

You will probably find this impossible. Stop and agree on some conventions for expressing some elements without telling the story.

Can you now convey the essence of the story? It need not be word for word. ◄

◄ Comment

(a) Some of the items will have been easier to convey than others—that is, when you could indicate an object

Δ by its shape: table
Δ by its movement: scissors
Δ by its position: sun
Δ as an activity carried out with it: telephone
Δ as one or more of its conventional attributes: man

Aeroplane could make use of several of these: position, shape and movement. Others would have been more difficult, particularly where it was harder to find specific attributes (apple, coffee) or where the notion itself was more abstract (mother, jealousy). For some you may have used signs similar to those of British Sign Language. These are illustrated in Figure 3.4 overleaf.

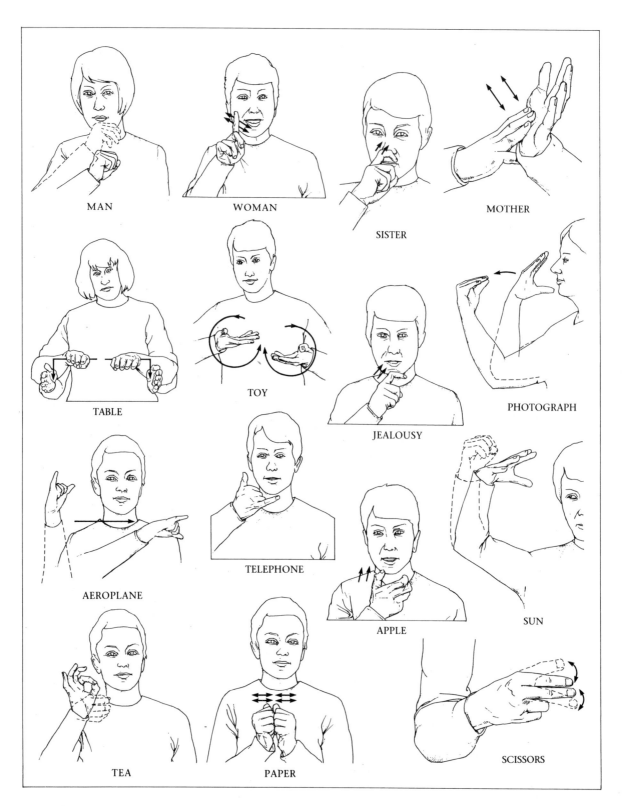

MAN

WOMAN

SISTER

MOTHER

TABLE

TOY

JEALOUSY

PHOTOGRAPH

AEROPLANE

TELEPHONE

APPLE

SUN

TEA

PAPER

SCISSORS

Figure 3.4

10

Even where this is the case it is important to note that these signs may not be universal, as Figure 3.5 illustrates.

(b) You will probably find this easier than the previous activity. You could have used position (or placement) as a major clue by drawing pictures in the air and indicating the part you wanted to refer to. You could narrow the search down by describing which room you were referring to before describing the particular object involved. You could specify not just the item itself but its relationship to other items.

(c) This exercise is very difficult. You will probably have found you needed to change the order of some elements to make it easier to convey the meaning: for example, to indicate 'wood' before describing going into it, to talk about the topic first. If you developed conventions, these may have particularly involved how to indicate time: for example, you may have indicated back in some way for the past, and forwards in some way for the future. Once you decided how to indicate 'tree', then 'taller' and 'close together' may have been easy. ◄

Many of the points emerging in these activities will be referred to later as we examine BSL in more detail. It is important to be clear at this stage that, while you were examining visual–gestural communication in some detail, this was a system of communication but in no way a language. It should have given you some ideas about the possibilities and constraints of gestural communication, which will help in understanding how British Sign Language works.

Figure 3.5

4 The structure of British Sign Language

This section of the course will serve different functions for different students, depending on whether you are a native user of BSL, have acquired or are acquiring it as a second language, or know no BSL at all.

British Sign Language has been defined as:

> ... a visual–gestural language used by many deaf people in Britain as their native language. The term 'visual–gestural' refers both to the perception and the production of BSL: it is produced on the hands and the rest of the body including the face.
>
> (Deuchar, 1984)

◀ Reading

The object of this unit is not to teach you sign language but to familiarize you with some of its properties.

You should now consult:

The Set Book by Miles, *British Sign Language: A Beginner's Guide*, Chapter 3 (pp. 44–106).

Reader Two, Article 6.1, 'British Sign Language: the Language of the Deaf Community' by Mary Brennan.

Through your reading you should make notes on the following:

Δ   the signing space
Δ   one-handed, two-handed and mixed signs
Δ   the hand: shape, position, orientation and movement
Δ   facial expression
Δ   bodily posture
Δ   placement
Δ   direction of signs
Δ   topic/comment structure
Δ   expression of time ◀

◀ Video

You should now look through Video Two and locate examples of all the different items specified in relation to the readings above. The *Video Handbook* indicates some, but you should be able to find others. You should consider which of these were important in your own attempts to communicate non-verbally and which were not. ◀

◀ Comment

We will not go through all the items here but discuss two to give some indication of the nature of BSL. Examples of all the features are given in the *Video Handbook* for Video Two.

Placement

A good example of the use of placement is found in the signing class in Sequence 2 of Video Two. It is important that, in describing in BSL the objects on the table, an indication of the precise location is given, while in English the speaker might just talk of a table with x, y, z on it.

In Activity 1(b) in Section 3, you may well have tried to introduce similar conventions to specify objects in the picture. However, the use of placement in BSL is much more complex than this, and is an integral part of the language.

Expression of time
Good examples of the expression of time occur in Sequence 4 at the LASER conference on Video Two, where participants speak of their past education, and their hopes for the future.

Time lines can be from front to back, across the front of the body or from the waist to shoulder. Although the majority of sign languages use time lines, they do not all use them in the same way. While in BSL the future is in front of the body, the past behind, in some other sign languages this is reversed. Rationales can be offered for both. In BSL and related sign languages, one can be seen as going forward into the future, leaving the past behind. The reverse view could be explained by suggestions that the past is in front because the past is known, or seen, whereas the future is behind because it is unknown, or unseen. ◄

5 Poetic form and sign language

The power and strength of BSL as a linguistic form can be seen in a number of different contexts. Unit 10 and Video Four will examine humour in BSL. Reader Two, Article 1.2 by Nora Groce, 'Everyone Here Spoke Sign Language', which you read in conjunction with Unit 1, looked at the power of sign language to express emotions. We shall take one further illustrative example here—poetic form and British Sign Language.

A poem can be defined as a 'composition in verse,[4] especially one that is characterized by a highly developed artistic form and by the use of heightened language and rhythm to express a highly imaginative interpretation of the subject' (*Random House Dictionary*).

By this definition, the potential for the creation of BSL poetry is tremendous, since the language itself constantly makes use of imaginative forms and rhythms. However, it must be remembered that, in discussing signed poetry, we are talking about performing it, since it has to be seen in action to be appreciated. This means that aspiring poets must also be performers.

The art of creating poetry for BSL has not yet developed as it should owing to lack of exposure to other original BSL poetry presentations and of training in the skills required, so that the history of signed poetry in Britain until recently had been mainly that of rendering English poetry in sign. In some cases, this poetry may have been original, but more often it has come from the printed book. Professionally, such renderings have often been, and still are, done in what is called sign-mime, a particular art form that resembles ballet in that the signs are often highly stylized (and frequently incomprehensible) and the signer makes minimal use of the mouth movements and facial expressions that are vital to everyday BSL.

[4]'That is, one that follows certain rules of arrangement' —Dorothy Miles.

What does go into signed poetry? Early research in the USA (Klima and Bellugi, 1979) has indicated some of the elements that may be present in either translated or original presentations. These may include the following (comments by Dorothy Miles are included in brackets):

Δ **Internal poetic structure.** This includes the choice of signs (particularly those with distinctive hand shapes, movements, and iconic structure), the rhythm and emphasis of these signs, and pausing.

Δ **External poetic structure.** Greater use of both hands to create a balance of left and right sides (including the use of simultaneity—a different image on each hand; and placement—where the images are positioned). Making signs flow from one to the other (where appropriate). Altering a sign, or one of its parts, to fit a pattern.

Δ **Superstructure.** A design in space made by the overall movement of the signs and locations where they are made.

These elements may not all be present in the signing of any particular poem, but are still valid in general.

In spite of the dearth of poems created for sign language in Britain, work elsewhere suggests that such poems may originate in several different ways:

Δ The poem may be written in English, with a choice of signs and rhythms that allow easy rendering in Sign Supported English (SSE). (Bilingual poet)

Δ The poem may be developed by combining strong images from sign language with equally strong images from English. An example of this is the poem *Total Communication*, by one of the authors of this unit (Dorothy Miles). Here the English phrase 'see eye to eye' is distorted into 'see aye to aye' where the sign language image is two heads confronting each other and nodding. Such a poem uses SSE with BSL borrowing. (Bilingual poet)

Δ The poem may be created in BSL (or ASL etc.) using the normal features of rhythms of the language, organized into the visual and rhythmic patterns described by Klima and Bellugi (1979) (BSL poet). It should be noted that many BSL stories are rendered in near-poetic form.

Δ The poem may be created from the distortion of the visual or rhythmic patterns of BSL—for example, done very quickly, with exaggerated movement etc. A remarkable version of *The Sorcerer's Apprentice* has been performed in this way.

A poem has been developed for the course by Dorothy Miles.

  ◀ Video
You should watch this poem now in Sequence 6 of Video Two. The **Video Handbook** includes an annotated version indicating the various features of BSL that it demonstrates. ◀

The English text of the poem is given below.

Art Gallery
I would like you to see this portrait
called 'Woman Seated'.
Notice the head, erect with strength and pride,
the face in repose, the eyes
dreamy, fixed upon the future
or on the past, perhaps:
notice the mouth, bravely sealed with a smile to show
she will never complain or cry out.

The chin
lifted, prepared to resist surprise ... or defeat.
See her shoulders, ready
to take on the burdens of the weak:
back straight, arms steady,
hands clasped in calm and patience.

The 'Woman Seated'
that you see here in this portrait
is a face well known.
People come to her and say,
'I know you,
I've seen you before', but she
is a portrait, flat, 2-D,
she cannot turn her head;
from her blank eyes she cannot see,
can't smile with warmth, can't speak; her fixed chin
can't lower or bend towards another.
She cannot hear, but cannot use her hands
to sign or shout or sing.

See now this woman standing,
Called 'A.N. Other'.
Notice the head bobs like a punch-ball:
the face is mobile, the eyes
seek for your glance, the mouth
often cries out and curses, but also laughs
at you and at herself.
The chin
constantly drops in wonder, awe, incredulity.
Shoulders and back already bowed
with her own burdens, she'll share
in those of others; arms weary,
but hands make constant effort
to sign and shout and sing.

She sings to try to please you.
She fears what you may feel.
And when in doubt she flees you.
Since she is not a portrait,
she is real.

(Dorothy S. Miles, November, 1989)

6 The recognition of British Sign Language

British Sign Language is one of the minority languages of Britain, and is probably used by at least 50,000[5] people as their only or preferred language, which is about one in 1,000 of the population. Comparisons with the extent of other minority languages in Britain are difficult, first because the necessary data are not available, and second because the basis on which comparisons could be made is unclear. For example, it is often stated that the second and third natural languages of Britain are Welsh, spoken by 50,000; and Scots Gaelic, spoken by 80,000–100,000. However, this may make for misleading comparisons as for many of these language users English will be their first language, unlike the majority of BSL users. The number of monoglot users of Welsh and Scots Gaelic is thought to be negligible, whereas for a substantial proportion of BSL users it is their only language. In addition, there are also many other languages in use in Britain—it is likely, for example, that the number of Urdu speakers exceeds the number of Welsh speakers, although figures are not available.

British Sign Language is becoming increasingly visible. Some television programmes have interpretation into BSL, and while the amount is still small, it is seen on some news programmes, specialist programmes for deaf people, in the signed interpretation of political party conferences and the Queen's speech at Christmas. Its identity as a unique language was only first established in October 1975 in a paper by Mary Brennan, published in the USA in the *American Annals of the Deaf*, which was re-published in this country in a supplement to *The British Deaf News* in February 1976.[6] She says:

> The discussion which follows will be concerned with so-called conventional or native-signing, i.e. with that communication system, which makes use of a set of directly semantic manual signs organised independently of English ... The abbreviation B.S.L. will be used for the abstraction 'British Sign Language' and A.S.L. for 'American Sign Language'. Although the use of these labels is primarily a matter of convenience, the incorporation of the term 'language' implies a theoretical position which will be expanded in the following pages.
>
> (Brennan, 1976)

This paper by Brennan was an important trigger for work in education and linguistics in this country. The first systematic study of BSL started at much the same time, by Margaret Deuchar who began her research in 1976. Deuchar had been influenced by work in the USA, where sign language research was already in progress. There the first person to focus attention on

---

[5] There has never been a complete survey and so figures for the numbers using the language are estimates and these vary. For example:

Deuchar (1984)	40,000
British Deaf Association (1987)	50,000
Sainsbury (1986)	70,000–80,000

[6] An earlier reference could possibly be identified in Stokoe's *Semiotics and Human Sign Languages*, 1972, where he refers to 'British Sign Language signers' on p. 121.

Figure 3.6
(Source: from *Illustrated London News*, 1865)

the systematic nature of sign language was Stokoe in his work on American Sign Language (ASL). In 1960, his paper, 'Sign Language Structure. Studies in Linguistics', was published in an obscure anthropological journal (Stokoe, 1960). This was a time of burgeoning interest in linguistics and languages and, as a result of this paper, Stokoe obtained money to do further research.

It is important to appreciate throughout this unit that the recognition of BSL as a language is very recent—and its history as an established language is very short. While the linguistic status of most languages can be taken for granted, for BSL it has been an issue which has dominated much of the research. This has implications for our wider study of Deaf culture, and will be important for our considerations of the role of sign language in education in Unit 5.

Of course, sign languages had been in existence long before they were identified and named as such. In Figure 3.6 the drawing from the *Illustrated London News* shows sign language in use at a gathering in 1865. From the earliest times there is evidence that communities of Deaf people used signing to communicate. One of the earliest references to signed communication is from Saint Augustine (AD 354–430) in Chapter 18 of *De Quantitate Animae Liber Unus*:

> Have you not then seen at Milan a youth most fair in form and most courteous in demeanour, who yet was as deaf and dumb to a such a degree that he could neither understand others nor communicate what he himself desired except by means of bodily movements?

For this man is very well known. And I myself know a certain peasant, a speaking man, who by a speaking wife had four or more sons and daughters ... who were deaf mutes. They were perceived to be mutes because they could not speak; and to be deaf also, because they understood only signs that could be perceived by eye.

The first documentation of sign languages is found in the books of Bulwer: *Chirologia: or the Natural Language of the Hand* (1644) and *Philocophus: or the Deaf and Dumb Man's Friend* (1648).

◀ Reading
Accounts of the early developments of signing are found in the two Set Books:

Sign Language: The Study of Deaf People and Their Language by Kyle and Woll, pp. 48–57;

British Sign Language: A Beginner's Guide by Miles, pp. 15–26.

And in Reader Two:

Article 6.2, 'Historical and Comparative Aspects of BSL' by Bencie Woll.

You should read these accounts now. ◀

Yet throughout history this signed communication was referred to as signing, or manual communication, or occasionally sign language (as a general term), rather than being specified as a language in its own right. Often discussion would even point out that signing was not a language—a point we shall return to later in Section 7. As late as April 1979, a seminar called to discuss 'Methods of Communication Currently Used in the Education of Deaf Children' had no reference to a British Sign Language but described signing variously as manualism, manual communication, manual systems and other terms largely including the word 'manual'.

ITQ
What are the implications of moving from terms such as 'manual methods' to British Sign Language? Consider this with respect to:

(a) the Deaf community; — *diff – separate –own lang*
(b) the educational establishment. *–less dep a Eng –ch—*

The use of the word 'language' implies a full communication system which has infinite possibilities. Dropping the term 'manual' means the language is not just conveyed by hands. For the Deaf community it means that their language is seen as a proper language and a matter of pride rather than as a debased method of communication. Deaf people can be considered as a linguistic minority group rather than as a group disabled by their limited communication. The term 'British Sign Language' could legitimate its use in education in a way that 'manual methods' does not. This is discussed further in Unit 5.

7 Myths and misconceptions about sign language

7.1 Popular misconceptions

Despite the systematic linguistic research on sign language since the late 1970s, many myths and misconceptions exist. Some of these are characterized in the following reviews of the BSL interpretation of the Queen's speech at Christmas in 1988. (We had hoped to include an excerpt of this on the video for the course but were unable to obtain permission.)

> The combination of noble Christmas traditions with the driving need to appeal to mass audiences produces a giddy merry-go-round of carol services and great music alternating with the tinsel and glitter of brash low comedy.
>
> Sometimes these two inimical strands tangled with each other in the same programme, the most remarkable of which was HM The Queen speaking to the Commonwealth. To see the collectors' item of the weekend you had to have watched it in its version for the deaf at 8.20 on BBC 2.
>
> Please do not write to tell me that I am guilty of irreverence to the Queen or lack of sympathy for the deaf when I tell you that I laughed so much that tears came to my eyes. It wasn't the fault of the Queen, who was frozen into her usual Christmas Day state of impenetrable dignity. It was the extraordinary woman they allowed to share the screen with her.
>
> This was a large blond lady in a blue dress who was busy translating Her Majesty's sober words into the wildest of sign language. She acted like an escapee from the Les Dawson Show. Her eyes rolled. Her mouth pulled itself into strange shapes. Her shoulders shrugged. Most baffling of all, her kaleidoscopic expressions seemed to have no relation to what the Queen was actually saying.
>
> Unfortunately she looked as though she were disrespectfully mugging and gesticulating over the Queen's shoulder while the Queen, sublimely unaware of her, acted as the straight man to her high comedy. This unintentional double act was the funniest 10 minutes of the weekend, but if I were the BBC executive, the sight of it would have ruined my Christmas.
>
> (*The Daily Telegraph*, 27 December 1988)[7]

> Which reminds me that the funniest thing I saw over the whole holiday period was the Queen's Speech as interpreted into sign-language by a splendid blond lady in a long blue dress. Her hands flew like birds to convey the message to the deaf, all the relevant emotions crossed her face in a constant flux of sun and cloud. It was an Oscar winner among sign–language mimes and nailed alongside her by the miracle of TV technology, the royal visage spoke and stared out in granite immobility. I hope HM and millions of the deaf enjoyed it

[7] Since this appeared, *The Daily Telegraph* has published an apology for its 'breach of taste'.

as much as we did. But my guess is some back-room electronic wizard is making urgent inquiries about emigration.

(*The Guardian*, 2 January 1989)

These convey a view that sign language consists of wild gesticulation, eyes rolling, mouth in strange shapes, shoulders shrugged and, furthermore, that sign language is a sort of mime. From your own observations and understanding it will be clear to you that such statements are a misrepresentation of sign language.

◀ Activity 2
In response to the two articles quoted above, write to *The Daily Telegraph* or *The Guardian*. ◀

◀ Comment
As well as distinguishing sign language from gesture and mime, you may have felt the need to comment on the attitudes to deafness and the Deaf community implied within these reviews. ◀

7.2 All sign languages are the same?

It is often assumed that there is only one sign language and that this is universal or international. Basically this is untrue. In Figure 3.5 you have already been introduced to the sign for MAN and WOMAN in a number of different languages, and it has been pointed out that ASL (American Sign Language) is not the same as BSL (British Sign Language). Interestingly, ASL shares more features with French Sign Language than with BSL, even though the USA and the UK share a common spoken language. This may be because the French sign language was introduced in the USA by the Frenchman Laurent Clerc who taught French Sign Language to Gallaudet and other pioneer teachers, and this had a major impact on American Sign Language. In Ireland too, there is a common spoken language but two sign languages. Irish Sign Language is used in the Republic of Ireland and by Catholic Deaf people in Northern Ireland, while British Sign Language is used by Protestant Deaf people in Northern Ireland. This distinction survives in Northern Ireland because Catholic and Protestant children are usually educated separately (Woll, 1988).

The reverse can also occur, in that two spoken language communities can share a sign language. In Belgium there is one sign language, although there are two spoken language communities, the French speaking and the Flemish speaking (Woll, 1988).

The idea that sign languages are universal may have arisen from the fact that Deaf people from different countries have a much greater facility to communicate with each other than do hearing people. This may be because Deaf people have a different approach to communicating, or have greater flexibility in their own language use. It may be that similarities in the structure of sign languages may facilitate communication across languages. Sachs (1989) suggests that while there is not a universal sign language, there may be universals *in* sign language:

> The hundreds of sign languages that have arisen spontaneously all over the world are as distinct and strongly differentiated as the world's range of spoken languages. There is no one universal sign language.

And yet there may be universals *in* signed languages, which help to make it possible for the users to understand one another far more quickly than users of unrelated spoken languages could understand each other. Thus a monolingual Japanese would be lost in Arkansas, as a monolingual American would be lost in rural Japan. But a deaf American can make contact relatively swiftly with his signing brothers in Japan, Russia, or Peru—he would hardly be lost at all. Signers (especially native signers) are adept at picking up, or at least understanding, other signed languages, in a way which one would never find among speakers (except, perhaps, in the most gifted). Some understanding will usually be established within minutes, accomplished mostly by gesture and mime (in which signers are extraordinarily proficient). By the end of a day, a grammarless pidgin will be established. And within three weeks, perhaps, the signer will possess a very reasonable knowledge of the other sign language, enough to allow detailed discussion on quite complex issues. There was an impressive example of this in August 1988, when the National Theatre of the Deaf visited Tokyo, and joined the Japan Theatre of the Deaf in a joint production. 'The deaf actors in the American and Japanese acting companies were soon chatting', reported David E. Sanger in the *New York Times* (August 19, 1988), 'and by late afternoon during one recent rehearsal it became clear they were already on each other's wavelengths'.

(Sachs, 1989)

However, we should not be deceived into thinking that sign languages are all the same—the need for many different sign language interpreters at international conferences for Deaf people is a sufficient indication of their diversity.

Figure 3.7   Interpretation at the International Congress on the Education of the Deaf, Manchester, 1985. Professor Harlan Lane speaking with American Sign Language, Swedish Sign Language and British Sign Language interpreters

(Source: courtesy of The British Deaf Association)

7.3 The iconic nature of sign language

In Section 2, one of the features of language described was the arbitrary nature of the linguistic element—that there was no direct relationship between the sign and word and that which they signified. One of the arguments that has been advanced against sign languages is that the signs are not truly arbitrary, but that there is a relationship between the sign and its meaning—that signs are iconic.

You will have realized from your own knowledge of BSL, or from trying to guess the meaning of signs for yourself, that a general relationship between the sign and its meaning is usually not immediately obvious, that signs are not transparent, although there are some that are. You will probably be able to guess the meaning of the signs in Figure 3.8:[8]

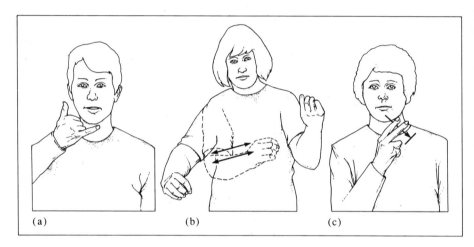

Figure 3.8

The next few in Figure 3.9 you probably cannot guess precisely, but once you know what they are you can make a connection between the sign and its meaning.

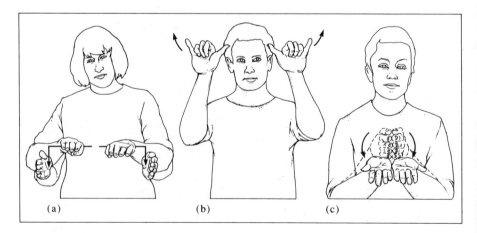

Figure 3.9

[8]The answers are given on page 53 at the end of this unit.

Klima and Bellugi (1979) have termed such signs translucent, where a relationship, while not transparent, can be derived between the sign and its meaning. That for a significant number of signs a relationship between the sign and its meaning can be described raises questions about the arbitrary nature of the linguistic elements of sign language.

◀ Reading
At this point you should read or re-read the following articles from Reader Two—they all discuss the iconicity of sign language. As you read them you should make notes on the following questions:

(a) Why should sign language be more iconic than spoken language?

(b) How does this reflect the status of sign language as a language?

Article 6.1, 'British Sign Language, the Language of the Deaf Community' by Mary Brennan;

Article 6.3, 'Sign Languages of Deaf People and Psycholinguistics' by A. Van Uden;

Article 6.4, 'Tell Me Where is Grammar Bred? "Critical Evaluation" or Another Chorus of "Come Back to Milano"?' by William Stokoe. ◀

It is probably the case that a greater proportion of the linguistic elements of sign language than of spoken language can be described iconically, though the figures given in the paper by Van Uden are probably overestimates—the generally quoted figures for iconic signs are between one-third and one-half (Bellugi and Klima, 1976: ASL; Deuchar, 1984: BSL; Boyes-Braem, 1986: general). For signs that are transparent, it is less than 10 per cent (Bellugi and Klima, 1976).

A number of points can be made:

Δ   Because sign language is a visual–gestural language, it lends itself more easily to iconicity. However, signs can only be iconic if they lend themselves to visual representation.

Δ   Some signs are iconic because of the conventional associations of meaning; thus, in BSL a sign involving the extended thumb usually has an element of 'good' in its meaning.

Δ   The iconicity is more pertinent to non-signers, particularly those learning to sign, than to native signers for whom the connections are irrelevant.

Δ   The iconicity of signs is often judged on isolated signs, which are modified in use.

Δ   Evidence from ASL shows that signs become less iconic over time.

Δ   While signs are iconic, they are iconic in different ways in different languages. BSL, Danish Sign Language and Chinese Sign Language all have an iconic sign for 'tree' but it is different in every case (Deuchar, 1984).

In focusing too closely on the iconicity of signs one can lose sight of the fact that it is the relationship of the signs to each other, and the structure of the language, which is also important, and which is discussed in the next section.

7.4 Sign language is not grammatical?

Much of the earlier work on BSL was to demonstrate that it showed the properties of a language, as, before the late 1970s and the beginning of systematic research on BSL, many asserted that it did not. Significant among these were eminent educationalists who were resisting the use of signing in schools:

> The signs in general do not follow a system of rules and therefore cannot be regarded as a language.
>
> > (Watson, Reader in Audiology and Education of the Deaf, 1967)

> The argument against the traditional sign language, that it is non-grammatical and impedes the development of correct language forms, is valid.
>
> > (Reeves, Headmaster, school for the deaf, 1976)

These, however, were written before the explosion of work on sign language which has increasingly demonstrated their syntax. However, there are still critics, of whom Van Uden is one of the main ones.

◀ Reading
You should now look *again* at the following two articles in Reader Two:

Article 6.3, 'Sign Languages of Deaf People and Psycholinguistics' by A. Van Uden;

Article 6.4, 'Tell Me Where is Grammar Bred? "Critical Evaluation" or Another Chorus of "Come Back to Milano"?' by William Stokoe. ◀

◀ Comment
Using the Stokoe article, and other material from this unit and Reader Two (particularly Article 6.1 by Brennan which you have already read), you should be able to develop your own arguments to support the view that sign language does have its own grammar. ◀

7.5 Sign language is a concrete language and cannot express complex ideas?

> ... I know this point of view is unpopular with many people—Sign Language is not 'up to it'. Signing can cope with everyday chat, but when it's necessary to get down to accurate reporting of specific terminology, signing breaks down. It hasn't the grammar and it hasn't the vocabulary.
>
> > (Firth, 1987)

> Pictorial thinking permits the deaf person to persist too long in a concrete sensual conception of happiness, and in doing so strengthens egocentricity. A pictorial way of thinking thus impedes an ascent to selfless love and authentic Christianity ... Now I am of the opinion that this pictorial thinking is especially heightened and established through sign language ...
>
> > (Van Uden, 1975)

24

◀ Activity 3

Prepare a response to the assertion that sign language can only express concrete ideas.

Sources:

1 Video One
Consider the ideas discussed in various conversations.

2 Video Two, Sequence 4.

This shows the 1989 LASER Conference (The Language of Sign as an Educational Resource). Some of the speakers are lecturing in BSL, others are lecturing in spoken English and are being interpreted into BSL (on the right of the screen—disregard the left which is Sign Supported English interpreting, to be discussed later).

3 Reader Two, Article 1.2, 'Everyone Here Spoke Sign Language' by Nora Groce.

In your reading of this article, note the number of different situations in which sign language was used. In particular, you may wish to comment that people would switch from spoken to sign language, and often the punch line of a joke was in sign language. Even if no Deaf people were present, hearing people might continue to use sign language if it was functional; for example, across great distances or noisy settings. For some situations—for example, preaching—sign language could sometimes seem more suitable.

4 Video Two, Sequence 6.

Dorothy Miles' poem in British Sign Language. The English version is reprinted in Section 5 of this unit. There are many other sources. Several of the articles in Reader One have been translated from BSL, and later videos contain discussions, sketches etc. You will notice that the dominant language of all of the videos is BSL. ◀

7.6 Sign languages are inferior to spoken languages?

One of the main ways in which sign language has been seen as deficient is through comparison with spoken language. It has been argued that BSL does not have the wide-ranging vocabulary of spoken English, nor the number of grammatical forms. It may be that sign language does not have the range of linguistic elements in some areas—in technology, for example, because this is an area to which Deaf people have not had access—but what is important is that, as with other living languages, BSL has the potential to develop vocabulary in an infinite number of ways. Among recent new signs are those for MINICOM (a visual telephone system), COMPUTER, CALCULATOR, TV PRESENTER, EDIT, RESEARCH.

The argument about limitations of the grammar is more complex and we would suggest that it arises in part from a particular research methodology. Some research on BSL has taken English as the standard and has then asked, 'How does BSL express that?'. Inevitably, this makes the comparison language seem inferior because there is no scope to demonstrate the strength of the language.

One area in which some linguists have pointed to sign language as being impoverished is in the expression of time relationships. In Activity 1(c) you were asked to work out ways of referring to the past and future using gesture. Some of you will have probably evolved a time line and then indicated the occurrence of events by indicating particular points on that line. This is a common way of talking about time in BSL. However, this creates difficulties in embedded sentences such as: 'Before he went shopping, John had a meeting with Mary, to finalize the arrangements for the following day'. It is important to realize that it is not that BSL cannot convey that information, but it would not use that type of sentence construction, which is English. An experimental set up which asked a BSL user to put across this message could make BSL seem very long-winded. Problems such as this arise when one language is taken as the base language, and much research into sign language is like this.

An example of an exception to this can be seen in the work of Miranda Pickersgill who examined in detail the way in which the sign usually glossed as 'FINISH' is used. The basic sign FINISH is illustrated in Figure 3.10.

Pickersgill's findings are based on observations of a man, deaf from birth and a fluent user of BSL, relying on observation on video recordings. Six main uses of the sign FINISH were identified, although most contained further possible subdivisions and could be utilized with differing emphases. They indicate that a British Sign Language user in signing FINISH has to show whether the completion is total or partial; whether there is personal involvement or it is the act itself which is significant; whether it is an individual act which is completed, or a sequence of acts; and whether the sign FINISH is used to imply that another related act will follow. The sign also has a use as an emphasis which may be stylistic and used more by some speakers than others. This is not to say that other languages cannot make such distinctions, but for many languages it is not required. Thus, a non-spoken language-centred approach can reveal a great deal about a language that is not immediately apparent from those approaches that take spoken language as their base line (Gregory and Pickersgill, 1988).

Harlan Lane (1985) has elaborated on the strengths of sign language by indicating the ease with which it expresses spatial concepts. He cites an experiment of his own based on ASL, in which pairs of students had to work with a dolls house. One had a photograph and had to instruct the other how to place seven pieces of furniture within the house. While speakers had to give elaborate explanations and had difficulty, ASL users could be much more economical in their descriptions and completed the task with comparative ease.

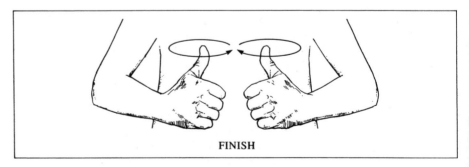

FINISH

Figure 3.10

7.7 Finger spelling and sign language

A further misconception, though of a different order, is that sign language is finger spelling—that is, spelling out the words by using a different hand shape for each letter—and many people have this idea.

While in Britain we use a two-handed finger-spelling system, in the USA and most other countries it is one-handed. Figure 3.11 illustrates the two-handed BSL alphabet and the one-handed ASL alphabet.

The Urdu alphabet and the Cyrillic alphabet of the USSR also have their own finger spelling as Figure 3.12 illustrates.

While finger spelling has a part to play in BSL, it is relatively small. Finger spelling is used for names and specialist words for which there is no sign available. Some signs, however, are based on letters of the alphabet. The sign for MOTHER is a double 'M', and for FATHER a double 'F'. Other signs in BSL incorporating letters are 'COLOUR', 'FAMILY', 'GOLD'. Letters may also be *combined* into signs. In BSL this occurs by a sequence of finger-spelt letters becoming the sign; for example, the BSL sign for Glasgow is G-W, and for Birmingham B-H-M. ASL can combine finger-spelt letters simultaneously. A classic example of this is the American sign 'I LOVE YOU' which Jimmy Carter made famous in his 1976 presidential campaign. This takes the ASL one-handed alphabet signs for I, L, Y and combines them into the sign 'I LOVE YOU', as Figures 3.13 and 3.14 show.

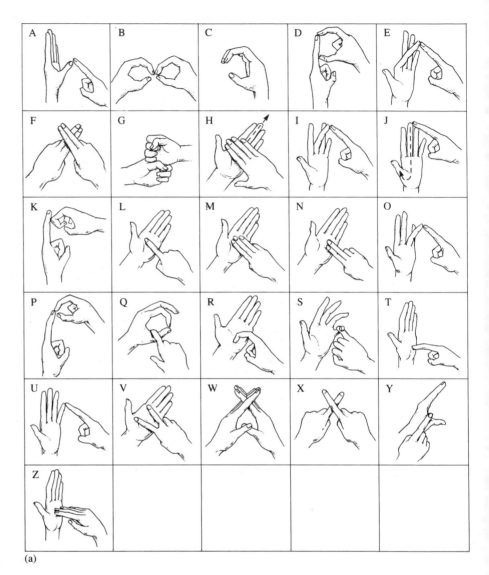

(a)

Figure 3.11   (a) BSL alphabet

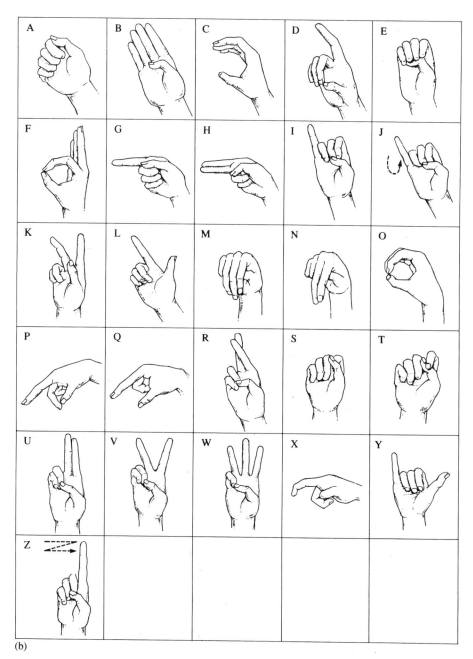

(b)

Figure 3.11　(b) ASL alphabet

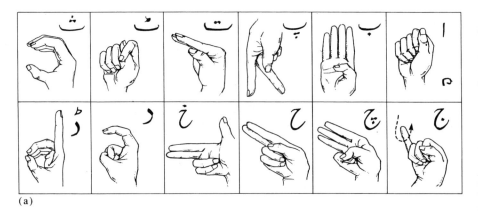

(a)

Figure 3.12   (a) Examples of Urdu finger spelling

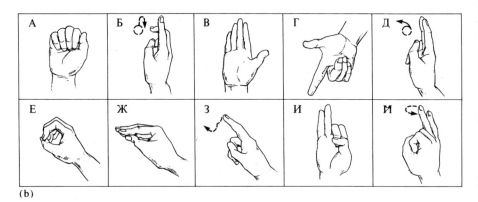

(b)

Figure 3.12   (b) Examples of Cyrillic finger spelling

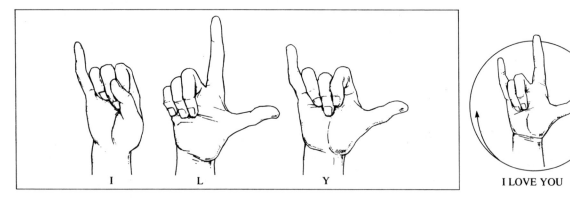

Figure 3.13

I LOVE YOU

Figure 3.14

◀ Activity 4

Learn the two-handed finger spelling system, or if you know the two-handed learn the one-handed.

For the two-handed start by learning A E I O U as illustrated in Figure 3.15.

Then gradually fill in the letters between.

You should achieve some competence in less than 30 minutes.

Use the following words for practice:

pig	jam	buzz
fun	hole	vest
dew	X-ray	quick

Ideally, you should persuade a friend to learn as well; while learning to finger spell letters is achieved relatively easily (although few non-native users achieve fluency), the reception or reading of finger spelling is much more difficult. Ask a friend to finger spell short words and try and read them. Identify particular points of ease and difficulty, and reflect upon any strategies that you develop. ◀

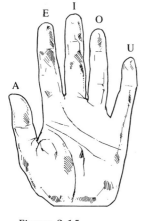

Figure 3.15

Finger spelling is rarely used as a total means of communication—clearly it would be very slow. If names are finger-spelt, when they are repeated this is generally reduced to the first letter of the name.

Some languages do include more finger-spelt words than others; traditionally, BSL in Scotland has incorporated more finger spelling, and occasional examples of total use of finger spelling have also emerged. Harold Hofsteater was born deaf to hearing parents who communicated with him totally using the one-handed alphabet. It is claimed he could read by the age of 4 years.

Communication with deaf-blind people is often totally finger spelt. In this country it is based on the two-handed alphabet, spelt on the person's hand (see Figure 3.16).

◀ Activity 5

Ask someone to learn a few letters from the deaf-blind alphabet, and to form words and spell them onto your hands.

(a) Can you read them?

(b) What are the difficulties? ◀

◀ Comment

(a) You will have found it much more difficult to read back finger-spelling than to do it.

(b) You will have tried to recognize individual letters—but this is too slow a process. Competency comes from recognizing groups of letters. ◀

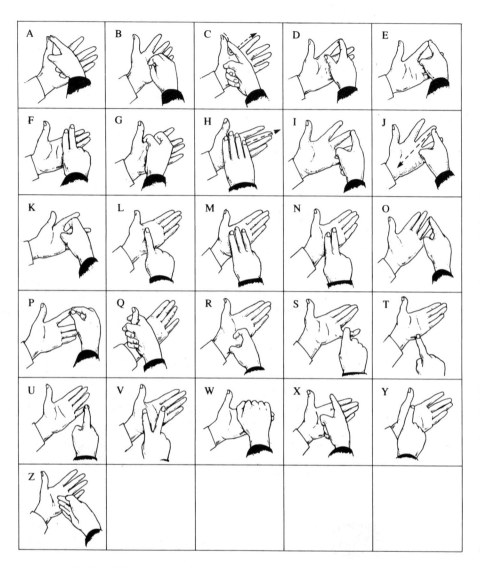

Figure 3.16   Deaf-blind manual alphabet

8 Signing in use: variations on a theme

8.1 Sign Supported English

Until now we have concentrated on BSL as the language of the Deaf community. However, many Deaf people use signs in a different way in that the signs, or the lexicon of BSL, are taken in conjunction with spoken English. In the UK, this is generally known as Sign Supported English (SSE). A few prefer the term 'Manually Coded English', though this is more widely used in the USA. Although 'Manually Coded English' emphasizes the English base of the language, the most commonly used term is Sign Supported English. SSE is communicating using spoken English (which may be voiced or not voiced) but introducing the lexicon of BSL to accompany the English. For a substantial number of deaf people, often those who were educated in spoken English or those who became deaf after acquiring speech, it is their preferred means of communication.

SSE is significant because it is the choice of most educators who advocate the use of signing in education, and until recently was the usual system for public interpretation into sign language. Also, until recently, SSE, because of its closer relationship with English, was seen as having a higher status than BSL. However, research on BSL, which has established it as a language in its own right, has done much to redress the balance.

8.2 Pidgins and creoles

When two languages come into contact, they influence each other. Usually one language is dominant, by reason of being used by the majority or the more forceful group, and this becomes the status language. Members of either group may learn the other language, but more usually they will learn only as much of the other vocabulary and grammar as they need for basic communication. The result is what we call a pidgin.

Where BSL and English are concerned, the situation is more complicated because deaf people are not homogeneous BSL users, and of those who do use BSL, few learned it as a native language (i.e. from their parents). Thus, the BSL/English pidgins should be seen as based on a continuum between the two languages, and people using sign may vary in their presentation along this continuum. Several terms have been created to name the various pidgins, and though these are not officially defined, some attempt to do so will be made here.

British Sign Language
British Sign Language is developed on visual–gestural principles. It borrows from English in using finger spelling, particularly for English personal names. Place names may be finger spelled too but often such finger spelling is done with a pattern that changes it to a sign. The signer may occasionally use an English-like mouth pattern, but the use of BSL patterns is more consistent.

Pidgin Sign Language

This pidgin makes more use of English mouth patterns to match individual signs with words, but still follows the grammatical structure of BSL. It is probably the most widely used pidgin among profoundly deaf persons.

Pidgin Sign English

Moving closer to English, this pidgin incorporates the structure of English into parts of its sentences, and the signer uses many English mouth patterns, but will also change in mid-sentence to BSL structures.

Sign Supported English

This is a form of visible English, in which the signer attempts to match English words with individual signs or finger spelling as closely as possible, often speaking at the same time. BSL features such as placement and classifiers may still be incorporated, but the emphasis is on the English word. This pidgin is particularly used by those who have lost their hearing after acquiring English, or who are speech-orientated by education.

English

The dominant language of Britain. A spoken language using minimal facial expression and few gestures.

It is possible to show these on a continuum:

British Sign Language	Pidgin Sign Language	Pidgin Sign English	Sign Supported English	English

Because the languages can be combined in this way (unlike spoken languages, although Franglais, in a trivial sense, might be considered similar), the form of sign language that is used between Deaf and hearing people may often be an adaptation, and not pure BSL.

Creoles

A creole occurs when a pidgin becomes the mother tongue of subsequent generations. Once this has occurred it develops in its own right, and syntax and vocabulary evolve. It has been argued that British Sign Language could usefully be considered a creole—Edwards and Ladd (1983) take West Indian Creole as a comparison and draw social and educational, as well as linguistic, parallels between the two languages. It has been suggested that because most deaf children are born to hearing parents, the creolization process takes place again for every generation.

8.3 Signed English

In Sign Supported English, not every single word or inflection (e.g. the 'ed' part of 'jumped' indicating the past tense) is represented by a sign. However, there have been attempts to represent English totally in sign. These have usually developed in an educational context and are known under the umbrella term of Signed English, although there are many varieties, including, in the USA, Signing Exact English (SEE) and Signing Essential English (SEEII). These are almost always developed by hearing people and rarely used by Deaf people.

8.4 Artificial sign systems

There are other artificial signing systems that have been deliberately created, usually for educational purposes. These include Cued Speech and Paget Gorman Signing System. Makaton is also used in education, generally with students with learning difficulties, and makes use of a limited number of BSL signs as part of a structured vocabulary used to facilitate language development. These are discussed further in Unit 5.

9 Sign language acquisition

9.1 Early studies of sign language acquisition

With the growth of interest in sign languages, people also became interested to see whether these were acquired in the same way as speech or in some different way. This section will look at the development of sign language in children acquiring it as their first language, usually deaf children of deaf parents.[9]

The early studies carried out in the 1970s, and mostly in the USA, were largely concerned to demonstrate that sign languages were not inferior to spoken languages and that children acquiring signs reached the same milestones at the same time as children learning to talk. This, of course, was at the time when people were concerned to establish the status of sign as a language. The studies were successful and, in fact, appear to indicate that signs were acquired earlier than speech. First signs were reported at an average age of 10.5 months (Schlesinger and Meadow, 1972) and 8.5 months (Bonvillian *et al.*, 1983), compared with an average for first words of hearing children at 11 to 14 months. Studies of sign language acquisition also report accelerated development through the second year of life with early two-sign combinations emerging before the average age of two-word combinations in children acquiring spoken language. Generally, two-word combinations occur at about 18 months of age. Two-sign combinations have been reported at an average age of 14 months (Schlesinger and Meadow, 1972) and at 17 months (Bonvillian *et al.*, 1983). Furthermore, other research shows that hearing children growing up in a bilingual speech/sign environment almost always sign before they speak.

While these studies may seem to show that sign is easier to acquire than speech, some caution must be shown in interpreting these results. They often fail to take account of the fact that for children developing sign as their first language their early gestures are considered part of their language development because they become incorporated into their later sign language, whereas with hearing children developing speech, their early gestural communication is disregarded.

[9]*Note:* The d/D distinction is dropped in this section, for the reasons described in Unit 1.

◄ Reading
You should now read the following article from Reader Two:

Article 6.5, 'What Sign Language Research Can Teach Us About Language Acquisition' by Virginia Volterra. ◄

The paper by Volterra in Reader Two concludes that, if gestural and spoken language are considered together, there is little difference between children acquiring sign language in homes where sign is the language of the home and hearing children acquiring spoken language. However, it is certainly clear from these studies that deaf children acquiring sign language are not at a disadvantage in their language acquisition at this stage when compared with hearing children acquiring spoken language.

9.2 How do children acquire language?

More recently, studies of language acquisition, both of sign and of speech, have been more concerned to describe *how* language is acquired—the process of language acquisition—rather than simply with establishing norms for various vocabulary sizes or word combinations. A number of factors have been important in such a shift of emphasis. First, there has been a growing realization that babies in the first 12 months of life are far more sophisticated than was previously thought. In particular, effective communications take place long before the beginnings of language; the child takes an active part in such dialogue and this prelinguistic period has been seen as crucial in the acquisition of language. Second, the work of the influential linguist, Chomsky, in the 1970s, on the structure of language gave rise to the question, 'How do children learn language from the language that they receive?'. This served to move attention to early interactions between child and adult rather than to focus on language production by the child. The study of sign language is clearly important for such work, and it is interesting to look at the similarities and differences between the acquisition of sign language and the acquisition of speech. The similarities are important because they reinforce the status of sign language as a language and, furthermore, can indicate basic universal properties in the acquisition of language. The differences are important in that they point to differences between visual–gestural communication and spoken communication.

9.3 Language acquisition by hearing children

There is a vast body of material on language acquisition by hearing children learning to talk, and in this section we shall highlight aspects of this to provide a framework in which to consider the language acquisition of deaf children. For hundreds of years the way in which children acquired language was not regarded as particularly complex. Children perceived an object, were told its name, and gradually built up a vocabulary of words by simple association. Saint Augustine described it thus:

When they named some object, and accordingly moved towards something, I saw this and I grasped that the thing was called by the sound they uttered when they meant to point it out. Thus as I heard words repeatedly used in their proper places in various sentences, I gradually learned to understand what objects they signified; and after I had trained my mouth to form these signs, I used them to express my own desires.

Yet, however this view of learning was elaborated and refined, it was unable to account for the learning of the structure of a language. Chomsky, in rejecting the behaviourist notions of language development, suggested that the structure of the brain makes us innately predisposed to learn language. Yet neither of these explanations seems adequate.

However, as has become apparent already from this unit, it is difficult to consider a language separately from its social context and, more recently, attention has focused on the wider social context of language learning in order to provide a richer model of the process. It is clear that language develops in a situation which is already meaningful, and in which the child is already able to communicate. Before children can talk or sign, they already have many of the skills necessary for later language development— they can take turns in interaction, they can request, they can indicate pleasure or frustration, and they can share a topic of attention. A recent focus of research on language acquisition has looked at the pre-speech period to try and evaluate the importance of pre-linguistic communication for later language development. It is in this area that the study of the acquisition of sign language could be particularly fruitful as the relationship of gesture to sign language is different from that of gesture to speech and it could illuminate an understanding of the relationship of linguistic to pre-linguistic communication. Whilst it is not possible here to provide a full account of language acquisition in hearing children, we would like to draw attention to specific aspects of the process.[10]

Before they are able to talk, babies can already make themselves understood and make sense of communications addressed to them. They are able to understand whether someone is pleased or angry with them. They will respond to particular remarks (either signed or spoken) such as 'I'm coming to get you', 'Where's teddy?', 'Leave that alone'. They are competent conversational partners taking turns in a conversation. The beginning of this can be observed in babies as young as 6 weeks of age. Later, in the second half of the first year of life, babies seem to engage in conversations in which their vocalizations sound like speech and may contain some close approximations to recognizable words, though they are not yet talking as such.

The role of the adult in developing communication skills is significant. Much adult talk to young children is about what the child is doing or looking at, commenting on the on-going activity. The talk is largely adapted to the child's linguistic competence—and 'motherese', or 'baby talk', has been extensively studied. At a simple level this may be the 'Gitchygitchygoo' utterances, which have useful intonation patterns for getting and maintaining attention. However, 'motherese' also refers to the simplification of speech, the shorter sentences and the reduction in grammatical complexity, which is a feature of speech to children.

[10] Students wishing to study this area more fully are recommended to consult Bruner (1983) and McShane (1980), though neither of these texts is essential reading for this course.

The important element of this is that much of the interaction takes place in already meaningful contexts. Many of the events of a baby's life—nappy changing, mealtimes etc.—are highly routinized and, later, ritualized repetitive games feature a great deal. While early approaches to adult–child interaction mostly looked at free play, essentially a novel situation, it now seems clear that routine provides a stable framework for the development of highly predictable interactions and, later, language.

9.4 Language acquisition by deaf children

From the description of language acquisition in hearing children it seems that, logically, there may be a problem for deaf children in that the visual channel has to be used for both the communication and the activity. In our description of hearing children much was made of the adult's comments on the child's on-going activity, and the place of games and ritual in language acquisition. Work on language acquisition of deaf children of hearing parents where speech was used seem to confirm these problems. It has been shown that turn-taking in interaction has been difficult to establish as measured by the high levels of vocal clashes where parent and child vocalize simultaneously and mothers report difficulties in playing anticipation games. It has also been shown that deaf children acquiring speech have fewer nominals (words that are used to name objects). This could reflect a difficulty in establishing joint reference where the mother names the object to which the child is attending. Also, the speech of hearing mothers does not show the same adjustment to the child's language competence.

Certainly deaf children of hearing parents have difficulty in acquiring language. In an interview study with over 100 parents of deaf children of less than 6 years of age, Gregory (1976) showed that in the group of 2 to $3\frac{1}{2}$-year-olds, only three out of twenty-seven could put words together into sentences and only six out of twenty-seven could understand people other than close relations or friends (see Tables 3.1 and 3.2).

Table 3.1   Language used by the deaf child, by age

Age (years)	Sentences	Language used		
		Over six words (not sentences)	Five or less words	No words
2.0–3.5	11% (3)*	19% (5)	33% (9)	37% (10)
3.6–4.11	21% (9)	38% (16)	21% (9)	19% (8)
5.0+	56% (19)	29% (10)	12% (4)	3% (1)
Total sample	25% (31)	25% (31)	25% (31)	24% (29)

* Figures in parentheses denote numbers out of total sample.

Table 3.2 People whose language is understood by the deaf child, by age

Age (years)	Almost anyone	People understood		
		Relations and friends	Mother only	No one
2.0–3.5	20% (6)*	15% (4)	37% (10)	26% (7)
3.6–4.11	29% (12)	38% (16)	19% (8)	14% (6)
5.0+	50% (17)	32% (11)	17% (6)	0% (0)
Total sample	30% (36)	25% (33)	25% (30)	19% (23)

* Figures in parentheses denote numbers out of total sample.
(Source: both Tables 3.1 and 3.2, Gregory, 1976)

A later, more detailed, study by Gregory and Mogford (1981) showed that deaf children being brought up through speech alone showed not only slower development but a different pattern of development—for example, they had different words in their early vocabularies to those of hearing children.

However, deaf children of deaf parents seem to acquire language at a more appropriate rate and informal observation shows that parents do not have the same difficulty with early communication skills. How then do mothers of deaf children establish pre-linguistic skills?

 ◀ Video
At this point you should look at the video of 2-year-old Ben (Video Two, Sequence 1) and comment on the communication. Ben and his mother (and also his brother and father) are deaf and the language of the home is BSL. Full information about this video is given in the *Video Handbook*. ◀

The problems reported for hearing mothers in establishing turn-taking with their deaf infants do not seem to be present for deaf mothers. Gregory and Barlow (1990) report in their study of deaf infants from 6 to 12 months that turn-taking with their deaf mothers is well established by that age. This seemed to be achieved by a slower pattern of interaction and thus there would be fewer turns in a given length of time than for hearing parents with hearing children. When deaf mothers wanted their child's attention they would usually indicate by touching the child but then wait for the child to look at them. Hearing mothers with deaf children often communicated when the child was not attending to them but to the toy, and would often disrupt the child's play to get attention.

Deaf mothers of deaf children also seem more tuned into their child's activities and more likely to comment about what he or she is doing. The study by Gregory and Barlow, already mentioned, found that 53 per cent of the comments of deaf mothers of 12-month-old deaf children was on what the child was doing, whereas the figure was only 26 per cent for hearing mothers. A more dramatic indication that deaf mothers are more tuned into their deaf child's activities comes from looking at the proportion of mothers' utterances unrelated to the deaf child's activities. This was 7 per cent of the total for deaf mothers, but 41 per cent for hearing mothers. Thus, while deaf mothers seemed able to make meaningful the child's activity, this was more difficult for hearing mothers.

For deaf children and their deaf parents, ritualized and anticipation games, which have a highly predictable structure, seemed easy to establish and were a feature of social play. Most deaf parents, in fact, seemed to have many such games that they enjoyed with their children. Thus, while hearing parents of deaf children report problems, this does not seem to be an issue for deaf parents.

As mentioned in Section 9.3, mothers' talk to hearing babies learning speech has been shown to be modified in that it has a simpler vocabulary and structure, sometimes known as 'baby-talk'. There is now evidence (from work in the USA) that there are parallels in the sign language use of deaf mothers to deaf babies. Erting reports:

> Deaf mothers modify the sign language they use with their infants, producing signs that appear slower, formatically different and grammatically less complex than the signing produced during adult directed discourse.
>
> (Erting, in press)

Erting also systematically looked at the sign for 'mother' (ASL) and found six differences in its form as used to babies acquiring sign and its adult use. These included being produced closer to the child, and being produced over a longer time by repeating the movement and thus allowing the child more time to see the sign.

However, there is another aspect to mothers' speech or sign to their deaf children. Compared with hearing mothers, deaf mothers speak/sign less often when they are playing with their children. Their spoken/signed utterances are much shorter, and there are many, many more repetitions. This has been reported in three separate studies (Woll *et al.*, 1988; Gregory and Barlow, 1990; Harris *et al.*, 1987).

ITQ

Why should deaf mothers use less speech/sign with their deaf children and include more repetition?

It is not clear why this should be the case, but it is interesting to speculate about the possible reasons:

1   It may be because activity has to cease or be suspended for communication to take place, because it uses the visual channel and deaf mothers are sensitive to a need for a slower pace of interaction.

2   It may be that the child has to look away from what he or she is doing for communication to take place, and these babies and young children need short relevant comments as they shift from toys to communication. Elaborated comments are only possible if they accompany the activity.

3   It may reflect cultural differences between the deaf and hearing community in the UK. Hearing communities differ vastly in the amount

40

they talk to young children, and it would not be surprising if there were differences between deaf and hearing mothers.

4 It could be an artefact of the experimental procedure which involved filming and recording mothers in interaction with their children. Deaf mothers and hearing mothers could respond differently to this situation, but it need not necessarily reflect differences in the way they interact with their children.

9.5 Advising hearing parents of deaf children

The studies reported above are clearly important in informing the understanding of language development in general, particularly that concerning the relationship of pre-linguistic to linguistic communication. However, these research studies are not just of academic interest but influence our thinking on how hearing parents of deaf children can best be advised about their child's language development. Should they be encouraged to sign to their children or to use spoken language? How best can they facilitate their child's language development? The vast majority of parents of deaf children will be hearing and until recently most will have been encouraged to aim for spoken language communication with their deaf children. However, the poor spoken language attainments of deaf children of hearing parents have led to increasing concern about the expectation that deaf children should develop spoken language first, particularly when deaf children acquiring sign do it so easily.

The findings concerning the success of deaf children of deaf parents have been used to argue that hearing parents should learn sign language and use it in communication with their children.

ITQ
What reasons can you give from what you have read, and from your own experience, for and against the idea that hearing parents should learn sign language to communicate with their deaf children?

In supporting the argument that parents of deaf children should learn to sign, you could have said:

1 Deaf children's sign language development is at least as good as hearing children's speech development, but deaf children learning spoken language are slower.

2 Sign language is the natural language of deaf people, in that it is the language most easily acquired.

Points to be made against this proposal could include:

1 Sign language is difficult to learn, and the parents would be acquiring language at the same time as the child and therefore would not be able to give the child a rich sample of the language.

2   It is very difficult for mothers to bring children up in a language that is not their own—mothers' talk to young children, or motherese, is a specialized way of communicating.

3   Deaf people might just be better at communicating with deaf children; it may have nothing to do with the use of sign language.

A great deal of advice is given to parents of young deaf children, much of it concerned with whether or not they should sign to their deaf children, and much of it contradictory. Consider these excerpts from two books for parents, both published in 1981 and still available and recommended:

> We strongly favour the Total Communication[11] position as a result of our interpretation of recent evidence. It is our opinion that the oral-only approach involves unnecessary and dangerous risks, because of its concentration on what the child cannot do (and is not likely to do). A solid educational approach requires, instead, an emphasis upon what the deaf child *can* do, recognizing his or her strengths as well as weaknesses.
>
> There is no way at present to predict which deaf children can be successful with an oral-only approach. Because sign languages have not been shown to affect negatively a child's chances of developing good speech, it seems vitally important to use signing as early as possible.
>
> (Freeman *et al.*, 1981)

> Many parents tell us that what they want for their child is for him to fit into society, to be acceptable socially; and paramount in their minds is that he should talk. For the great majority of hearing impaired children this is possible, given that they are provided with an environment where at the early stages the only form of communication is through spoken language, and later through spoken and written language. Success depends further on emphasising normal standards in behaviour (as we describe in this book), work and play, as well as normal standards of communication; and it also depends on the fullest and most efficient use of what remaining hearing the child has.
>
> We would argue that the language of hearing impaired children suffers delays related to an absence of early stimulation, but that once started, and provided sufficient stimulation is given, it follows a pattern very similar to the language development of normally hearing children.
>
> (Nolan and Tucker, 1981. This book was revised and re-issued in 1988; however, this section remained the same)

Both books give seemingly clear unequivocal advice—yet it is totally contradictory.[12] The problem arises partly in the different interpretations given to research findings, for, while the advice is clear, the evidence on which it is based is complex. At first sight, the fact that deaf parents are

---

[11] Total Communication is an approach using signs and speech together. This is discussed in more detail in Unit 5.

[12] The different ideologies underlying such advice are considered further in Unit 8.

more successful in communicating with their deaf children would seem to imply that the answer lies in sign language. However, not all deaf mothers sign to their deaf children—in the study by Gregory and Barlow (1990) one-third used oral communication. These mothers were as successful in establishing communication as those who signed. While many would consider that it is an indictment of the oral education that the parents received themselves, that the parents feel spoken language is superior and the language they should use with their deaf children, this is nevertheless a factor in the consideration of the advice that should be offered.

Moreover, even those who use BSL did not introduce it until after the first year (about 15–18 months), and they used vocalization, touch and some gesture before that. The usual reason given was that they did not use sign until the child was ready, which meant able to sign back (Woll *et al.*, 1988; Gregory and Barlow, 1990).

If the pre-linguistic period is important for later language development, it may then be that the skill of deaf parents lies in establishing good pre-language communication with their deaf children, rather than in signing *per se*. If this is the case, it is not an argument for or against signing. There is yet another factor—even if signing itself is not important, it may be good advice to encourage hearing parents to sign because signing to their deaf children may in turn encourage them to communicate overall in a more appropriate way. There is, of course, a more general issue as well—that for a parent to learn to sign and to use sign language is an indication of an attitude to Deaf people and their language, which is significant beyond the immediate language-learning context. Some deaf young people welcomed their hearing parents' attempts to learn sign language for this reason, rather than for any improvement in communication that took place as a consequence.

◀ Reading
You should read Article 5, 'Total Commitment to Total Communication' by Riki Kittel, and Article 7, 'Deafness: the Treatment' by Lorraine Fletcher in Reader One. These relate to early stages of the authors' children's language development, and the decisions they made. ◀

10 Teaching and assessing British Sign Language

While children seem to acquire BSL easily and naturally, the issue for adults, as in the acquisition of any other language, seems more complicated. Until recently there was little formal teaching of BSL, and most hearing people who knew BSL were hearing children of Deaf parents, or adults who had continued contact with Deaf people in the context of their work.

In the 1970s, interest in sign languages resulted in a demand for signing classes which were almost entirely organized by hearing people. These hearing people obviously would not be trained in sign language teaching and, moreover, foreign language teaching at that time was formal and usually grammar based. Often the signing classes were spoken language based and signs were given for each individual word, which was a completely inappropriate way to teach BSL and resulted in the acquisition of a signed form of English, rather than BSL with its own grammar. There was little systematic thought on the teaching of sign, and items such as finger spelling races were often a feature of such classes.

More recently, Deaf people have become involved in the teaching and the assessing of sign language skills through the British Sign Language Training Agency (BSLTA), now the British Sign Language Tutor Training Course, and the Council for the Advancement of Communication with Deaf People (CACDP).[13]

Figure 3.17   A sign language class being taught by a BSLTA-trained tutor (Source: courtesy of Terry Boyle, photographer)

◀ Reading
From Reader Two you should now look at:

Article 6.6, 'A Stimulus to Learning, a Measure of Ability' by T. Stewart Simpson;

Article 6.7, 'British Sign Language Tutor Training Course' by A. Clark Denmark. ◀

Clark Denmark's article describes the setting up of a course for training Deaf people to teach BSL. A striking point about the tutor training itself, and the material developed for tutors to use with students, is the emphasis on BSL throughout. Thus, there is little written material, and essays and examinations are submitted on video.

[13] The Scottish equivalent of CACDP is SASLI—the Scottish Association of Sign Language Interpreters. Its predecessor, SAID—the Scottish Association for Interpreting for the Deaf—did much of the pioneer work in this area.

◀ Video

You should now watch Video Two, Sequence 2, where you will see such a class in action. The tutor is Deaf, the students hearing and it is only their sixth lesson, so you should follow most of the class. The *Video Handbook* gives further details of the session. ◀

◀ Activity 6

You should consider advantages and disadvantages of the method employed in the tutor training.

In Stewart Simpson's article you read about the development of the assessment of sign language skills and, more generally, communication with Deaf people. In considering this article you should note how Deaf people have become involved in the assessment, and the implication of this. ◀

◀ Video

Sequence 3 on Video Two shows an assessor in training. The *Video Handbook* gives further details of the session. ◀

Both the articles by Simpson and Denmark and the two video sequences you have just seen have emphasized the emerging role of Deaf people in teaching and assessment. It has clearly not always been the case that Deaf people have had this role, as such teaching and evaluation of signing skills as occurred before were clearly the prerogative of hearing people. Moreover, aspects of the organization and assessment still seem to be located in the hearing world.

ITQ

What are the implications for the Deaf community of their increasing involvement in sign language teaching and assessment? — *their own lang incl*

What further developments would you like to see? *respons create new*

11 Sign language interpreters

As you will have read, part of the original impetus for CACDP was to establish a register of sign language interpreters. This was part of a move to put interpreting on a more professional basis. In the past, Deaf people generally used friends and relations to interpret for them in dealings with hearing people. For many Deaf people, the informal network of help is still important in providing interpreter support. Sainsbury (1986), in her interview study of 175 Deaf people, found that one-third used relatives as interpreters, a quarter used Deaf friends and a sixth used hearing friends. Of the formal support, the Social Worker with Deaf People was most commonly used, though interestingly a number of other professionals had been called upon: Citizens Advice Bureaux, police and general practitioners. There is now a move to separate interpreting from social work services for reasons to be discussed in Unit 7.

Deaf people are now expecting more of interpreters, and are beginning to recognize good interpretation as a right not a favour. The article opposite by Peter Jackson in *The British Deaf News*, September 1986, attracted a great deal of correspondence, and we also include here two of those letters.

◀ Activity 7

You should watch again Video Two, Sequence 4, dealing with the LASER conference. This time you need not be concerned about the content but concentrate on the process of interpreting.

(a) The spoken language was interpreted into Sign Supported English and BSL. How do these differ?

(b) How does interpreting between speech and sign differ from interpreting between two spoken languages? In thinking about this it will be useful to consider a specific example of interpretation between two spoken languages—for example, a Gorbachev–Thatcher meeting. ◀

◀ Comment

(a) (i) Sign Supported English follows the spoken English more closely in time while BSL lags behind the speech, because the interpreter has to process chunks of the language before interpreting it.

(ii) BSL needs less finger spelling.

(iii) There is more use of body movement and facial expression in the BSL interpretation.

(b) (i) The sign language interpreter has to be visible, whereas an interpreter for spoken languages does not. Even in spoken language interpretation, where the interpreter is visible, he or she is usually in the background, while in sign language interpretation the interpreter has to be prominent, be placed in a good light etc.

(ii) In the face-to-face situation, the sign language interpreting can be, and often is, simultaneous because it uses a different modality for communication. In spoken language it has to be sequential. This does not apply to spoken language outside the face-to-face situation—for example, at conferences where the interpretation is relayed through headphones and participants watch the speaker but hear the interpreter.

(iii) While it is not integral to the situation, different practices have arisen with sign language and spoken language interpreters. A sign language interpreter often acts for both participants, interpreting speech to sign and sign to speech, and often it is made explicit that his or her responsibility is to both groups. In spoken language interpretation the interpreter is usually only responsible to one group, and is thus distanced from the role of mediating between the two groups. ◀

The profession of interpreter for Deaf people is still very young, but is growing. Training is being developed, although the requirements are still not as high as for spoken language interpreters. This is not to say there are no very highly skilled interpreters, rather that they are in short supply which puts them in a very powerful position.

COMMENT

Since I became Allan Hayhurst Research Fellow, I have been to numerous conferences, seminars and workshops at which there has been a presence of deaf people. Most of these deaf people come in two categories—deaf "professionals" who work full-time in deaf-related employment and the "voluntary deaf", deaf people who do not hold paid employment in the deaf world but who are heavily involved in a voluntary capacity, and who are interested in broadening their knowledge.

It would seem to me that the presence of such deaf persons ever should be actively welcomed. Indeed, many hearing professionals do welcome their presence. BUT, are these deaf people being treated fairly in one area—that of the provision of interpreting sevices?

There seems to be a number of organisations around that appear to have a total disregard for the interpreting needs of deaf people attending conferences, seminars and the like. Major organisations like the BDA take these interpreting needs seriously, but too many appear to feel that so long as they can get someone along who can sign a bit, they have taken care of this aspect. The end result—as I have seen several times—is often that the conference/seminar degenerates into disorder. A workshop that I attended in July which attracted a good number of deaf people (my estimate is that a third of those present were deaf) really took the biscuit and earns from me the dubious honour of being the worst ever conference/seminar/workshop that I have had the misfortune to attend, due to the total disregard of the need for competent interpreters.

The advance programme for this workshop excited a lot of interest, and looked certain to be of a high standard, yet on the day the programme was ruined because the organisers did not take into consideration the need

for a couple of interpreters recognised as being proficient at this level of communication.

It would appear to me that they were waiting to see who turned up on the day in the hope that there would be some who could do an adequate job of interpreting. As it happened, two of the country's top-class interpreters DID turn up—IN THEIR OWN PRIVATE CAPACITY AS OBSERVERS AT THE WORKSHOP. They WERE asked to interpret, and they REFUSED.

And most deaf people present accepted and respected their decision! Why?

Because they knew that the organisers were trying to cater for deaf people's needs on the cheap by not appointing proper conference interpreters; that the organisers were relying on people taking pity on the deaf observers frustration to volunteer their services as interpreters. In fact, two persons who had only just passed CACDP's Stage 3 Communication Skills course did take over as interpreters, and did their best. It was not always good enough, especially during voice-overs, and hearing people in the audience could not help being aware of this. Nonetheless, the deaf observers appreciated these two ladies' efforts. BUT it should never have happened.

By not appointing interpreters recognised at this level, the organisers were not only abusing deaf people's needs but were also abusing the needs of hearing people in the audience who, because of their limited or non-specialist contact with deaf people, could not follow Sign Language and relied on voice-overs, AND had to suffer constant interruptions for clarification by the interpreters trying to translate difficult pieces into Sign Language.

Though this article refers to one recent workshop, other organisers need not be complacent just because no-one has complained in writing about their own seminar/conference etc.

To conclude, organisers of any

conference of whatever nature should always prepare for the needs of deaf observers AND hearing observers through voice-over interpretation, and be prepared to pay for the service. It is simply not good enough to rely on whoever turns up and hope they will interpret. To be a conference interpreter takes special skills over and above normal stage 3 communication standards.

There was, I feel, some unfair criticism of CACDP during one point in the workshop. However, I do feel that CACDP should be getting together with SAID (Scottish Association of Interpreters for the Deaf) and set up a separate register of CONFERENCE interpreters—at present, probably no more than 20 exist in the country.
P.W. Jackson

Dear Editor,

I wish to congratulate Peter Jackson for his most excellent Comment (Sept. 1986, p. 5) on conference interpreting.

While I fully endorse what he had to say, I wish to add my view that not only is there a great need for improved conference interpreting services, deaf participants must learn to speak out their objection or dissatisfaction at low quality of interpreting services provided for them. I don't mean that they should wait till after a speaker finishes his speech or after a conference/seminar/workshop ends before informing the organisers; instead they must learn to 'voice' their opinions at any point of conference/seminar/workshop proceedings so that the organisers can change an inferior interpreter for a better one immediately and then the deaf participants can follow the conference/seminar/workshop better.

My following experience illustrates this: I attended a workshop ironically organised by the same people who organised the York workshop to which Peter Jackson referred in his article and there was an interesting talk entitled "Legal Rights of the Deaf". However, my husband and I were unable to follow the talk because an interpreter, who was a

trainee, was very obviously struggling to do his job. As minutes sped by, we decided not to wait 'till the speaker finished before requesting the organisers to switch interpreters; otherwise we would miss the whole speech and we could not very well ask the speaker to repeat for us and other deaf participants. So at our request, the organisers switched interpreters, though somewhat reluctantly, and at the end of the day we were amazed to find little support from other participants (deaf and hearing) for our action. This incident in fact occurred three years ago and from Peter's article it is evident that the York workshop organisers have not learned their lessons yet.

There is definitely a great need for deaf consumers to be educated on how to use interpreters and how to 'voice' their complaints/objections to inferior services.
Lilian K. Lawson

Dear Editor,

I am glad that Lilian Lawson had the courage to speak out about the lamentable standard of interpreting at some public meetings. Our Annual Meeting was held in September and we asked for a first class reverse interpreter so that our deaf members could speak freely and the hearing people could understand and join in the debates. But the voice-over was so bad that hardly anything the deaf said was understood and a social worker sitting at the back had to give a running commentary to the hearing people.

I feel extremely angry when I see this happening as the job of the interpreter is to form a bridge between the BSL of the deaf speaker and the English of the hearing people. We need more than good interpreters—we need first-class reverse interpreters who can make deaf people feel at home in any situation.
Bob McCullough

(Sources: Jackson, 1986; Lawson, 1986; McCullough, 1987)

12 Language and power

In Section 8 on language use by deaf people, it was pointed out that different forms of a language have different statuses—that a language can have both a high and a low form which are held in differing esteem. This does not apply just to different forms of the same language—throughout history different languages have carried different statuses. In the Middle Ages Latin was spoken by the higher classes, and schoolboys could be expected to speak Latin in the playground as well as in the classroom. In 1677, undergraduates at Queens College, Cambridge were instructed to speak Latin in Hall, and as late as the nineteenth century there was a scandal at the University of Leiden in Holland when a new professor gave his inaugural lecture in Dutch and not in Latin.

Other languages have also been afforded a high status at different times in history. In medieval and early modern Europe, French was the language of the élite, spoken at various times in England, Italy, Prussia and in Russia as late as the nineteenth century. A way of colonizing the world or of extending one's power base was in the extension of the use of one's language. Queen Catherine of Spain, when she sent her ships out, gave her officers the command to teach Spanish to all with whom they came into contact.

In contrast to languages held in high esteem, other languages were held in low esteem or were actively suppressed. Throughout history the suppression or the marginalization of languages of minority groups has been a means of oppression. In the UK, some minority languages have had to fight for recognition. Welsh was given equal status with English (but only in Wales) by the Welsh Language Act of 1967. This gives the right to present evidence in Welsh in a court of law, to communicate with government bodies in Welsh and to publish statutes in Welsh. Scots Gaelic was spoken by 300,000 people in 1800, but the number has now dropped to less than 100,000. The creation of the Western Isles Council in 1975 gave rise to a revival of interest in the language and by 1980 an official bilingual policy was in force, though English remains the dominant language.

Sign language too, has been suppressed and ignored. Emphasis has been made in this unit on the struggle for sign languages to be recognized as legitimate languages, yet, despite all the work done on sign language in this country, it still is not recognized as an official language of the UK. However, the European Parliament has given its support for the recognition of the sign languages of the member states, as the title, shown opposite, of an article which appeared in *The British Deaf News* of July 1988, demonstrates. The nature of this recognition is set out in full in the EEC document reproduced on page 50.

In 1989, at the ECRS[14] fifth Annual Conference in Brussels, the sign language interpreters were paid at the same rate as the spoken language interpreters. However, at the time of writing (1989), and for the first time since 1981, there was not one sign language interpreter at the Conservative Party conference in the UK, although this matter has now been resolved and there will be in future.

---

[14] ECRS: The European Community Regional Secretariat of the World Federation of the Deaf. This is a non-government organization consisting of the national associations of the Deaf in the European Community, and was established in 1986.

Euro' parliament gives its total support for the recognition of Sign Languages

(Source: *The British Deaf News*, July 1988, vol. 19, no. 7)

In the UK itself, however, British Sign Language is not yet recognized as an official language. While this may not seem significant, it can indeed be so. For example, the Central Council for Education and Training in Social Work (CCETSW) mentions signing in its equal opportunities policy: '... that individuals are not unfairly disadvantaged on the grounds of language (including sign language) ...' (CCETSW Council meeting, 16 June 1989).

However, this language policy applies only to Welsh and English, as the two official UK languages:

> The Council noted that English and Welsh are the two official UK languages and approved the principles and the main components of a policy on the Welsh language following recommendations from the Committee in Wales. The principles, as amended are:
>
> (1) A client has a basic right to choose the language of interaction with the social work agency and its workers and there is therefore a consequent need for social workers and care workers who can offer a professional service through the medium of Welsh in all parts of Wales.
>
> (2) CCETSW should promote and encourage equal status for the Welsh and English languages in its work in Wales.
>
> (3) CCETSW should seek to ensure that Welsh medium education and training is available for students who wish to study and practice in Welsh, and that English medium education and training is culturally and linguistically sensitive.
>
> (CCETSW Council meeting, 16 June 1989)

How significant a step it would be if BSL had the same recognition!

Harlan Lane argues vividly that the suppression of sign language and the failure to use it as a language of education is a major contribution to the suppression of Deaf culture in this country, as well as in the USA and other European countries. He says:

> Few communities have as long and as tragic a history of language oppression, however, as deaf communities in the Western World. Many centuries went by before the world even recognised manual languages. ... Today, more than a century since the Congress of Milan, the oppression of the languages of deaf communities in Europe and America continues unabated and in the crucial realm of education that oppression is becoming worse.
>
> (Lane, 1985)

REGULATION ON THE OFFICIAL RECOGNITION FOR SIGN LANGUAGES

The European Parliament

— having regard to the fact that deaf people should have the same right as other people to participate in and contribute to all aspects of economic and social life,

— having regard to the fact that deaf people should be given every opportunity to lead as independent a life as possible,

— having regard to the 500,000 profoundly deaf people in Member States whose first language is their national Sign Language and not the dominant mother tongue of their country,

— having regard to the fact that profoundly deaf people, being born deaf or becoming so in early childhood, are unable to understand speech with or without the use of a hearing aid and, as a consequence, are unable to acquire the use of speech naturally,

— having regard to the status of Sign Language as a visual gestural language, recognised as a language by linguists, that is based on the hands, arms, eyes, face and body, and incorporating the use of finger-spelling, which is the manual representation of the written alphabet,

— having regard to the non-universality of Sign Language and that deaf people of one country use a different Sign Language from deaf people of another country,

— having regard to the vital importance of access to a language, which offers the ability to communicate effectively, to understand and be understood,

— having regard to the right of every deaf person to choose the most suitable method of communication, whether it be a sign language or a spoken language,

— having regard to the fact that Sign Language is a living language and is constantly changing to meet the needs of modern society,

— having regard to the fundamental importance of the role of the National Associations of the Deaf in Member states, in representing and protecting deaf people and the vital part they play in the training of Sign Language interpreters,

— having regard to the importance of deaf people themselves being given the opportunity and means by which to teach their national Sign Language to others,

— having regard to the essential role of Sign Language interpreters for deaf and hearing people alike, and specifically their role in facilitating the access of deaf people to information, appropriate education, health provision, professional employment, culture, leisure opportunities, the media and in day-to-day life as citizens,

— having regard to the shortage of trained Sign Language tutors, assessors and interpreters, due, for example, to the lack of resources within the National Associations for their provision, and their lack of status in terms of training and professional practice,

— having regard to the fact that Sign Language is totally compatible with other methods of communication in education, and is the only possible means of communication between parents and their child before the latter has acquired the use of a written/spoken language,

— having regard to the great number of young deaf people in Member States denied Sign Language, who have to leave school without qualifications and a reading age of eight and three-quarter years with unintelligible speech, and poor lipreading abilities, and whose lack of qualifications greatly reduces job prospects and career potential, and literally denies them a voice, and opportunities for integration in society,

— having regard to the fact that use of Sign Language is not in any way an obstacle to the participation of deaf people in our society,

A. deeply concerned that the Governments of Member States have taken no positive steps to grant to their deaf communities the same rights and opportunities as the dominant hearing communities, to grant recognition for the distinct Sign Languages of deaf communities of Member States, also that the necessary resources are not made available to the National Associations of the Deaf for the training of Sign Language teachers and interpreters in order to promote a better cultural and social life for deaf people in Member States,

B. recognising that access to the information of a society is a right of all deaf people,

C. having regard to the contribution deaf people can make to society,

D. concerned that the absence of official recognition for Sign Language has meant that it is not sufficiently used in education, within the family with a deaf child or adult, in job training, on television, in the theatre, or at public meetings,

1. Welcomes the concern expressed by the Community's Bureau for Action in Favour of Disabled People, Commission for Employment and Social Affairs,

2. Welcomes the proposal of the Youth, Culture, Education, Information and Sport Committee,

3. Calls on the Commission to put forward a recommendation for the Council to agree on the implementation of a regulation to Member States to grant official recognition for the Sign Languages used by deaf people in those States,

4. Calls on the Council to ensure that the national governments of Member States abolish any obstacle preventing the use of Sign Language,

5. Calls on the Council to make available funds through the Community Social Fund for training a sufficient number of Sign Language tutors, assessors and interpreters in Member States,

6. Calls on the Council to make available funds to promote the publication of a Sign Language dictionary in each Member State,

7. Calls on the Council to make available further funds to the Community's Bureau for Action in Favour of Disabled People, Commission for Employment and Social Affairs, for the development of services for deaf people in Member States.

(Source: European Parliament, UK Office)

He quotes the first president of the National Association of the Deaf, Robert McGregor, writing at the turn of the century:

> What heinous crime have the deaf been guilty of that their language should be prosecuted? ... The utmost extreme to which tyranny can go when its nailed hand descends upon a conquered people is the proscription of their national language. ... By whom then are the signs proscribed? By ... educators of the deaf ... by a few philanthropists ... by parents ... worst of all these (people) ignore the deaf themselves in their senseless and mischievous propaganda against signs. Professing to have no object in view but the benefit of the deaf, they exhibit an abject contempt for the opinions, the wishes, the desires of the deaf.
>
> (Ibid.)

Beyond the suppression of the language, or the failure to recognize it, languages can be defined as inferior or inadequate. This allegation is made about sign language with respect to its lack of written form, which, it is argued, makes it inferior. These arguments have been particularly rehearsed in the area of education.

ITQ

Make notes on the way in which written language can be seen as different from spoken language. In what ways do they differ from each other?

In answer to this ITQ, you could have suggested:

1 Written language is usually more grammatically correct than spoken language.
2 Written language is more explicit. In speech the context is often relied upon, whereas written messages are more explicit.
3 Written language is generally acquired after speech.
4 More developed languages usually have a written form whereas more primitive languages rely only on speech.
5 Written language is more binding in that it gives a permanent record whereas speech does not.

The comments given above represent the types of conventional statements often introduced in order to assert the superiority of written language over speech. Some writers have claimed that the development of literacy within a culture is related to the development of higher thought processes and it has been suggested that literate cultures are more sophisticated. This view arises partly from the fact that the usual way of studying a language is to examine its written form, and speech is often evaluated by how closely it corresponds to the written language. Recently, such views have been challenged[15] and speech and writing each considered as important in their own right.

[15] These points are fully discussed in Street (1984).

Writing is only more grammatically correct than speech if it is taken as the standard, and speech compared with it. The correctness of speech is actually judged in a different way from that of written text. It would be incorrect to utter sentences as they would be written. Usually, written language is more explicit because it occurs in situations in which it has to be—where the context does not support the meaning. Occasionally, of course, we write notes to each other, where meaning relates to the situation, and in such instances the language we use is different. Like writing, speech can also be very flexible. It may also be totally explicit, and in formal situations such as speeches, lectures and sermons, it usually is.

The argument over which is the more binding is interesting. While it seems clear to us that the written record is more permanent and thus more binding, it has not always been the case. As people became more literate, speech was still seen as creating a more binding agreement because once said it could not be changed—whereas writing could. Written records were often seen as more suspect, perhaps because people were less likely to trust the unfamiliar medium. A parallel to this may be seen in discussions over evidence to be presented to courts. There is a reluctance to accept video recordings of interviews with children (which has been recommended in child abuse cases) because courts feel that they are more likely to get at the truth by having the witness present.

Thus, the notion that a language needs to have a written form and is somehow inferior without it is challenged. Yet the notion that some languages are superior to others means that some languages are marginalized and this process itself is important. Notions of language and power have been a recurring theme throughout this unit, as they will be throughout the course. In this unit we have suggested the power of language in the description of communities and of languages, and the power of the use of language to construct and maintain particular power relationships. In Unit 4 we look at other groups of deaf people and how their 'otherness' is created. The following three units look at deaf people in a hearing world, and the issue of language will be pertinent to all of these. We will return to review issues of language and power in Unit 8.

Suggestions for further reading

The two Set Books for the course provide excellent further reading:

KYLE, J. and WOLL, B. (1985) *Sign Language: The Study of Deaf People and Their Language*, Cambridge, Cambridge University Press.

MILES, D. (1988) *British Sign Language: A Beginner's Guide*, London, BBC Books (BBC Enterprises).

Aside from the section in Dorothy Miles' book specifically referred to in Section 4 of this unit, both of these books are recommended for further reading. They provide interesting discussion of many of the issues discussed in this unit.

For those wishing to look at a linguistic account of British Sign Language, a good introduction is:

DEUCHAR, M. (1984) *British Sign Language*, London, Routledge and Kegan Paul.

The more general issues of language and power (though not specifically sign language) are discussed in:

ANDERSON, R. (1988) *The Power and the Word*, London, Paladin.

Answers for page 22

Figure 3.8

(a) Telephone

(b) Violin

(c) Cigarette/Smoking

Figure 3.9

(a) Table

(b) Cow

(c) Book

References

BELLUGI, U. and KLIMA, E.S. (1976) 'Two faces of sign: iconic and abstract', *Annals of the New York Academy of Sciences*, no. 280, pp. 514–38.

BONVILLIAN, J.D., ORLANSKY, M.D. and NOVAK, L.L. (1983) 'Early sign language acquisition and its relation to cognitive and motor development', in Kyle, J.G. and Woll, B. (eds) *Language in Sign*, London, Croom Helm.

BOYES-BRAEM, P. (1986) 'Two aspects of psycholinguistic research: iconicity and temporal structure', in Tervoort, B. (ed.) *Signs of Life: Proceedings of the Second European Congress on Sign Language Research*, Amsterdam, The Dutch Foundation for the Deaf and Hearing Impaired Child, The Institute of General Linguistics of the University of Amsterdam, The Dutch Council of the Deaf; Institute publication no. 50.

BRENNAN, M. (1976) 'Can deaf children acquire language?', Supplement to *The British Deaf News*, February.

BRENNAN, M. (1987) 'British Sign Language: the language of the Deaf community', in Gregory, S. and Hartley, G.M. (eds) (1990) *Constructing Deafness*, London, Pinter Publishers. (D251 Reader Two, Article 6.1)

BRITISH DEAF ASSOCIATION (1987) 'The case for BSL. BSL and Britain's minority languages', *The British Deaf News*, vol. 18, no. 9, September.

BRUNER, J. (1983) *Child's Talk: Learning to Use Language*, Oxford, Oxford University Press.

BULWER, J.B. (1644) *Chirologia: or the Natural Language of the Hand*, London, R. Whitaker.

BULWER, J.B. (1648) *Philocophus: or the Deaf and Dumb Man's Friend*, London, Humphrey Moseley.

DENMARK, A.C. (1990) 'British Sign Language tutor training course', in Gregory, S. and Hartley, G.M. (eds) (1990) *Constructing Deafness*, London, Pinter Publishers. (D251 Reader Two, Article 6.7)

DEUCHAR, M. (1984) *British Sign Language*, London, Routledge and Kegan Paul.

EDWARDS, V. and LADD, P. (1983) 'British sign language and West Indian creole', in Kyle, J. and Woll, B. (eds) *Language in Sign*, London, Croom Helm.

ERTING, C. (in press) 'The interactional context of deaf mother/infant interaction', in Volterra, V. and Erting, C.J. (eds) *From Gesture to Language in Hearing and Deaf Children*, Heidelberg, Springer-Verlag.

FIRTH, G. (1987) Letter, *The British Deaf News*, January.

FLETCHER, L. (1987) 'Deafness: the treatment', in Taylor, G. and Bishop, J. (eds) (1990) *Being Deaf: The Experience of Deafness*, London, Pinter Publishers. (D251 Reader One, Article 7)

FREEMAN, R.D., CARBIN, C.F. and BOESE, R.J. (1981) *Can't Your Child Hear?* London, Croom Helm.

FURTH, H.G. (1973) *Deafness and Learning: a Psychosocial Approach*, Belmont, CA, Wadsworth.

GREGORY, S. (1976) *The Deaf Child and His Family*, London, George Allen and Unwin.

GREGORY, S. and BARLOW, S. (1990) 'Interaction between deaf babies and deaf and hearing mothers' in Woll, B. (ed.) *Language Development and Sign Language*, Bristol, Centre for Deaf Studies.

GREGORY, S. and HARTLEY, G. (eds) (1990) *Constructing Deafness*, London, Pinter Publishers. (D251 Reader Two).

GREGORY, S. and MOGFORD, K. (1981) 'Early language development in deaf children', in Kyle, J.K., Woll, B. and Deuchar, M. (eds) *Perspectives on British Sign Language and Deafness*, London, Croom Helm.

GREGORY, S. and PICKERSGILL, M. (1988) 'Temporal reference in British Sign Language', Paper presented at the Third European Conference of Developmental Psychology, Budapest, June.

GROCE, N.E. (1985) 'Everyone here spoke sign language', in Gregory, S. and Hartley, G.M. (eds) (1990) *Constructing Deafness*, London, Pinter Publishers. (D251 Reader Two, Article 1.2)

HARRIS, M., CLIBBENS, J., CHASIN, J. and TIBBITTS, R. (1987) 'The social context of early sign language development', Paper presented at the *Child Language Seminar*, York.

HARRIS, R. (1980) *The Language Makers*, London, Duckworth.

JACKSON, P.W. (1986) *Comment, The British Deaf News,* vol. 17, no. 9, September.

KANNAPELL, B. (1980) 'Personal awareness and advances in the Deaf Community', in Baker, C. and Battison, R. (eds) *Sign Language and the Deaf Community,* Silver Spring, MD, National Association of the Deaf.

KITTEL, R. (1989) 'Total commitment to total communication', in Taylor, G. and Bishop, J. (eds) (1990) *Being Deaf: The Experience of Deafness,* London, Pinter Publishers. (D251 Reader One, Article 5)

KLIMA, E.S. and BELLUGI, U. (1979) *The Signs of Language,* Cambridge, MA, Harvard University Press.

KYLE, J.G. and WOLL, B. (1985) *Sign Language: The Study of Deaf People and Their Language,* Cambridge, Cambridge University Press. (D251 Set Book)

LANE, H. (1985) 'On language, power and the deaf', Address to Manchester Deaf Club on the occasion of the *International Congress on the Education of the Deaf.*

LAWSON, L.K. (1986) Letter in *The British Deaf News,* vol. 17, no. 11, November.

MCCULLOUGH, B. (1987) Letter in *The British Deaf News,* January.

MCSHANE, J. (1980) *Learning to Talk,* Cambridge, Cambridge University Press.

MILES, D. (1988) *British Sign Language: A Beginner's Guide,* London, BBC Books (BBC Enterprises). (D251 Set Book)

NOLAN, M. and TUCKER, J. (1981) *The Hearing Impaired Child and the Family,* London, Souvenir Press.

Random House Dictionary (1967) Stein, J. (ed.), New York, Random House Inc., p.1110.

REEVES, J.K. (1976) 'The whole personality approach to oralism in the education of the Deaf', in *Methods of Communication Currently Used in the Education of Deaf Children,* London, Royal National Institute for the Deaf.

SACHS, O. (1989) *Seeing Voices,* London, Picador.

SAINSBURY, S. (1986) *Deaf Worlds,* London, Hutchinson.

SCHLESINGER, H. and MEADOW, K. (1972) *Sound and Sign: Childhood Deafness and Mental Health,* Berkeley, CA, University of California Press.

SIMPSON, T.S. (1990) 'A stimulus to learning, a measure of ability', in Gregory, S. and Hartley, G.M. (eds) (1990) *Constructing Deafness,* London, Pinter Publishers. (D251 Reader Two, Article 6.6)

STOKOE, W.C. (1960) *Sign Language Structure. Studies in Linguistics,* Occasional Paper no. 8, University of Buffalo.

STOKOE, W.C. (1972) *Semiotics and Human Sign Languages,* The Hague, Maitor.

STOKOE, W. (1987) 'Tell me where is grammar bred? "Critical evaluation" or another chorus of "Come back to Milano"?', in Gregory, S. and Hartley, G.M. (eds) (1990) *Constructing Deafness,* London, Pinter Publishers. (D251 Reader Two, Article 6.4)

STREET, B. (1984) *Literacy in Theory and Practice,* Cambridge, Cambridge University Press.

TAYLOR, G. and BISHOP, J. (eds) (1990) *Being Deaf: The Experience of Deafness,* London, Pinter Publishers. (D251 Reader One)

VAN UDEN, A. (1975) 'Religion and language in the pre-lingual deaf', in Pokorny, D.H. (ed.) *My Eyes Are My Ears*, a collection of papers delivered at the *lst International Ecumenical Seminar on the Pastoral Care of the Deaf.*

VAN UDEN, A. (1986) 'Sign languages of Deaf people and psycholinguistics', in Gregory, S. and Hartley, G.M. (eds) (1990) *Constructing Deafness*, London, Pinter Publishers. (D251 Reader Two, Article 6.3)

VOLTERRA, V. (1986) 'What sign language research can teach us about language acquisition', in Gregory, S. and Hartley, G.M. (eds) (1990) *Constructing Deafness*, London, Pinter Publishers. (D251 Reader Two, Article 6.5)

WATSON, T.J. (1967) *The Education of Hearing Handicapped Children*, Manchester, Manchester University Press.

WOLL, B. (1987) 'Historical and comparative aspects of British Sign Language', in Gregory, S. and Hartley, G.M. (eds) (1990) *Constructing Deafness*, London, Pinter Publishers. (D251 Reader Two, Article 6.2)

WOLL, B. (1988) 'Report on a Survey of Sign Language Interpreter Training and the Provision within Member Nations of the European Community', *Babel*, vol. 34, no. 3.

WOLL, B., KYLE, J.G. AND ACKERMAN, J. (1988) 'Assessing sign language acquisition', Paper presented at the BATOD/NCST meeting, Birmingham, 12 March 1988. Copies available from the Centre for Deaf Studies, University of Bristol.

WOOLF, V. (1967) 'On being ill', in Woolf, V. *Collected Essays*, vol. 4, New York, Harcourt.

Acknowledgements

Grateful acknowledgement is made to the following sources for permission to reproduce material in this unit:

Text

Jackson, P.W. (1986) *Comment* from *The British Deaf News*, vol. 17, no. 9, September 1986, reproduced by permission of The British Deaf Association; *REGULATION on the Official Recognition for Sign Languages*, European Parliament, UK Office, reproduced by permission.

Tables

Tables 3.1 and 3.2 Gregory, S. *The Deaf Child and His Family*, George Allen and Unwin, 1976, reproduced by permission of Unwin Hyman Ltd.

Figures

Figure 3.7 copyright © by The British Deaf Association; *Figure 3.17* copyright © by Terry Boyle, photographer.

Grateful acknowledgement is made to Trevor Landell for permission to use his painting on the covers and title pages throughout the units of this course.

We are also grateful to Laraine Callow for advice on the sign language illustrations.

Figure 3.3(b)